CONSCIOUSNESS IS UNDER THE RUBBLE

A Guide to Unpacking Childhood Trauma and Unleashing Your Inner Power

Penny Payton & Vincent Wiggins, EdD

CONTENTS

Introduction.. 1

Introducing The Authors.. 8

Penny Payton 9

Vincent Wiggins, EdD 12

Part One: The Indoctrination Loop Of Unawareness. 14

Chapter One: What Is Self-Awareness? 15

Chapter Two: The Big Disconnect. 24

Chapter Three: Life By Default. 34

Chapter Four: An Open-Minded Pursuit Of The Truth. 41

Chapter Five: Living Within The Flow Of Life........... 48

Chapter Six: Breaking Down The Barriers. 51

Part Two: Building And Maintaining Emotional Self- Awareness In Professional And Personal Environments: Tools, Strategies, And Exercises. 57

Chapter Seven: Understanding ARMS. 58

Chapter Eight: Assess 61

Chapter Nine: Reflection. 65

Chapter Ten: Manage... 72

Chapter Eleven: Support. 77

Chapter Twelve: ARMS for others. 80

Part Three: Hope For The Future, From Clueless To Conscious. 86

Chapter Thirteen: Evolution Is A Lifelong Process..... 87

Chapter Fourteen: Social Consciousness. 92

Moving Ahead 96

Quick Reference Vocabulary Guide 98

Suggested Readings. 100

References 101

Books By This Author 103

Introduction

D id you know that there are experiences from your childhood that are holding you back? Yes, it's true! Now don't put the book down or look around like you were not meant to read this. It's for you. This book has been written with every single person in mind because no one has been excluded from the effects of their childhood. This might be something that hasn't crossed your mind. Often it takes a major occurrence for a person to become introspective. Now, as mental health and childhood trauma have become more mainstream topics, it truly can benefit us all to look inward.

Childhood and trauma are two words that sound both sad and frightening when used together. But if we take a little time to understand it a bit more we can learn how it applies to us all, especially in the settings of our adult lives today. In childhood, at our most vulnerable as our smallest and youngest selves, the tiniest of things can feel and seem extremely frightening. Or painful. Or confusing. Those feelings, when left unexamined or unexplained, creep into our subconscious and hunker down. Initially we are too young to notice or know what to do but emotions will continue to be repressed when we don't gain the tools or guidance to navigate them properly. Sadly, our caregivers may not have been taught to be emotionally aware either.

This is why childhood has been the hidden factor in how we all live our lives and the effect we each have on the world. Within the years of our childhood experiences, as we move from infant through to adult, we are in learning mode. We learn through all of our senses and all of our experiences. We primarily learn the most from our caregivers, which makes us limited to their knowledge base when it comes to the most important human factor: emotional competency. While other people may also have an impact, we will naturally defer to those who we count on most for our survival.

The level of emotional self-awareness of our care givers will greatly impact our entire lifetimes. It is their actions that (inadvertently) create the most significant trauma we carry forward. In the past trauma was more often thought of as the big stuff. However, those are the things that usually get the proper attention and go on to be processed and released.

As we live our adult lives it ends up being the small hidden things that matter the most as those have the deepest impact - whether we know it or not. Each of us has been left unaware that our emotional self- awareness have been compromised to some degree, not just by trauma but by conditioning as well. By learning more about our past we can turn the tables and use these specific instances to our advantage for change and growth. As we examine our childhood experiences and remove the baggage our emotional self-awareness and consciousness will increase, along with sustainable happiness and inner peace.

To be conscious we need to be able to both acknowledge and take responsibility for our own emotions, while allowing others to do the same. For some that might start by first accepting emotions have any real value in life. The levels of emotional self-awareness each of us experience can be considered to be on a spectrum which is based on two things: your upbringing and the level of introspective work you've completed thus far. As mentioned, for many of us that has been little to none; and in most cases, we've not been given the proper tools to understand how emotions work at all.

For many the first priority in life is to stay in forward motion, which leaves little room for introspection. Most of us have learned to become externally focused. At the same time, a deeper part of ourselves, our souls will continually call us back home (inward) to our own truths. This is the conflict of balance. Not work/life balance, but true personal internal/external balance. This is why our efforts to find sustainable peace and happiness don't work. We can't find balance by always being in forward motion and externally focused, especially when the answers for our own behavior can only be found within.

We all have an inkling that there is more to life than how we live it. There is always something we'd like to change in our lives. Everyone has had moments we've looked back on conversations and questioned what we've said. And a lot of us have behaviors we simply cannot control no matter how hard we try. We all have that one thing. It can change but there is always something.

Those are the sparks that are calling us home to a better way forward. Those are the moments that point out our internal disconnection. Our souls all seek healing and balance. Within every drive for success, we will find a desire for peace. Within even our strongest connections we feel the need for freedom.

How often do your best efforts fail to produce the lasting results you desire? Why do self-help books pile up in the corner either unread and abandoned, or having brought no lasting change after reading them? We mistake the use of retail therapy as the freedom to buy what we want even though it further imprisons us at our jobs; just as the overuse of comfort foods makes us that much more uncomfortable in our bodies.

It's not in the minutes spent in meditation or yoga where deep sustainable inner peace is found. It's found by going inward toward a much deeper personal understanding of ourselves and what constructed our beliefs, perspectives, and values in life. This is where inner peace begins to be cultivated, by looking inward to understand how and why the issues blocking our power were created.

Unfortunately, most all of us were discouraged from looking deeply inward, and instead taught to ignore our own emotions for the most part. Without knowing what else to do, we repeatedly seek. In the deepest crevasses of our hearts, we just want our issues to go away. We make excuses. We may even exchange one obsessive behavior for another. Sometimes we even give up, but the sense of needing to do better, be better and find a better way does not relent.

So, get out a journal or open your laptop and start making notes right now about things that bother you or things you'd like to change because we will do work around it in part two. Give it a name. Admit it's your current nemesis. Because that thing right there, it's your best friend. It's your ticket inside. It will open the door to things you've never imagined possible. Why? Because that thing is in direct conflict with your soul's natural quest for peace and happiness.

By continually seeking answers from the outside, we give our power to others. Our pain is a big money maker. Throughout this book as we gain the tools to manage emotions fully and uncover our hidden pain points we can explore ways to finally gain more personal control, because getting to the truth about yourself is what matters most. That's where you go back to your natural way of life, that's where you find your soul again. Here we will explore what we consider to be the three stages of moving toward a life more fulfilled: Indoctrination, Awareness, and Consciousness.

How to prepare for this book

Any journey of self-exploration is bound to evoke some strong emotions. Emotional work can be trying at the best of times, exhausting at the worst. For this reason, let's start with a very basic understanding of how emotions are meant to work. Our emotions really can be our best friend and trusted guide throughout life, but without understanding them properly we can easily begin to ignore ourselves in ways we generally won't notice.

CONSCIOUSNESS IS UNDER THE RUBBLE

Unfortunately, we learn subliminally through messaging that our emotions are to be ignored, distrusted, and even feared. This means we often ignore most of the indicators we get from them because we have not learned how to understand their meaning. As a result, we are left in a state of confusion and distrust ourselves because we lack a solid foundation of emotional awareness.

Emotions affect us differently based on our experiences, both past and present. And the levels of personal safety we have come to feel internally. For many, emotions can feel overly important. They can be so overwhelming that they will be internalized and have more meaning attached than a situation needs, which can make everything feel extremely personal. This is natural and will feel normal if your emotions were ignored in your childhood.

Someone else may be able to look at a similar situation and compartmentalize or deflect the emotion, seemingly giving it no meaning at all. Neither of these opposite ends of this spectrum are the path to a balanced or healthy emotional state of conscious awareness.

Knowing where you fall within that spectrum is important because it will help you determine your level of emotional self-awareness. (A survey is available at www.unpackingemotionalbaggage.com).

Common terms for describing emotional baggage such as broken, brokenness or damage can provoke pain and cause shame. Especially considering our state of emotional awareness was developed during childhood. To prevent further harm let's consider that we are not damaged goods. Instead, we were untrained, sometimes neglected or abused and so were our caregivers. As we move through these chapters you will learn more about the fact that none of this was originally your fault.

We all carry hidden pain from the past. This book is meant to be an overview and an exploratory guide, but some of you may want to start digging in too, so as you move through this reading it's important to remember that you are safe. Find or create a safe space within your current life where you can relax and breathe in peace and solitude when you need to. If feelings of panic arise, or something becomes overly emotional, remember it's just an emotion. It's a feeling about something that has happened before. It just needs to be acknowledged and managed properly. You can choose to not let it carry you away from safety. We provide a free course, also found a www.unpackingemotionalbaggage.com, which we will reference again later. This should be reviewed as you begin this journey, and at any time needed as you proceed.

The goal is to find the best way for you to navigate this work without being overwhelmed. If you need the help of a professional do not hesitate to find one. Engage those that you can emotionally trust beforehand, so you have support along the way if that's what you need. Journaling about your experiences can be an excellent way to sort out your own emotions and free space in your mind to move ahead. Each of us has lived with our emotions compartmentalized and bottled up in some way for decades. So please be gentle and cautious as we begin to understand and unravel them safely.

The book is divided into three parts. Part One examines the indoctrination phase of life. Part Two consists of exercises intended to raise emotional self-awareness. Part Three is about raising consciousness on both personal and global levels.

As a precursor to this book, one of the authors has shared her own journey towards emotional self-awareness in a book titled Unpacking Emotional Baggage which you may find to be a useful read as you start uncovering your own story.

Author's notes: A pound to a Penny

My "one thing" that was my lifelong nemesis was food and weight. In the back of my mind, no matter how much I weighed I would hear myself say "I need to lose weight". My obsessive behavior was compulsive binge eating. I started researching this ten years ago, before childhood trauma was making headlines and triggers were even discussed. I thought some parasite overtook my brain and forced me into the ice cream section at the grocery.

I did my work with the help of hypnotherapy and uncovered about a million pain points. I was aware my childhood was kind of wonky, but I had no idea exactly just how isolated, neglected and emotionally abused I had been.

I became a mom at eighteen, far too young and without uncovering any of my repressed trauma. My son became a victim of trauma too. Trauma can happen when your parents love you deeply. It can happen when you are the most important thing in their lives. It happens because emotions have been shoved under the rug for generations. It happens because our parents didn't know how to get in touch with ourselves.

I used to shrug things off as personality traits (not knowing they are not fixed). I used to think of myself as an emotional person (and couldn't recognize that I lacked emotional awareness). And I was absolutely certain I knew what I was doing and what was best for everyone else most of the time. I was positive I was doing a better job of parenting that my parents had. Learning the truth and unraveling those outdated perspectives changed my entire life. I hope you will take a journey inward to change yours too.

Introducing The Authors

We put the author section up front because we are two passionate people on a mission to raise consciousness globally. By sharing and teaching what we've learned over the course of a decade of dedicated investigative research and experiences, we find that increased emotional self-awareness is crucial to personal empowerment and strong leadership, personally and professionally. Individuals who self-reflect and reevaluate become far more conscious than those who do not. Parts of what we share have been proven in other fields of study and some are just emerging. We believe you will find the combination of materials presented here to be the most thought-provoking to date.

Penny Payton

This book, as was my first book, has been a labor of love sparked by a growing concern for the fate of humanity. I feel a deep calling to help. With each increase in emotional self-awareness, we move into greater consciousness globally. Interest in self-healing is already starting to become the new norm. These books were created after I experienced the profound benefits of my own introspective healing work.

This, however, has not always been my passion. For over 50 years, I lived a very different life; a financially lucrative one that I believed to be going just as planned. If anyone would have told me that I had experienced something that sounded as serious as generational childhood trauma, I would have laughed out loud. In fact, it's possible that many people believe the same of their lives, too. It wasn't until my life collapsed after a neardeath experience that I started looking at everything very differently.

Like many, I have battled with my weight all my life, and that's where my new journey began. As I deconstructed my family's generational trauma I was shocked by what I found. The most damaging trauma is the sneaky, subtle, and continued messaging we receive as kids, which is why many remain unaware of its existence or impact. But it was in those experiences that the cause of my own dysfunctional behavior was rooted. By paying attention to the triggers, I experienced I exposed the repressed energy that led to my finding the cause of my battle with food and weight. By processing and releasing that energy, I overcame my dysfunctional addiction.

After a decade spent out of the workplace consumed in research, determined to release every single piece of emotional baggage that I carried, I found complete and total success, (along with some other amazing things). These experiences prove it to be possible to attain self-efficacy when it comes to addictions. It became clear how little we humans know about the massive impact childhood has on our adult lives. Or just how important it is for this information to become public. Which is why we are introducing this more in-depth material informed from my own experiences and discoveries.

Today, I speak with people regularly who have come from loving homes and have wonderful relationships with their parents. They are often financially successful. But they all have repeated patterns in their lives they'd like to stop. They all want more freedom, more peace, and, of course, more happiness. They are all basically the old version of me. And they too are always shocked by how much we uncover in just one conversation, by looking to those years for the answers.

I wasn't always the author of my own story. My drive was based in pursuit of an external means of success. I carried the false belief that the internal always worked itself out. Like magic or something. I thought my relationships were successful when they suffered from disconnect, because I was totally disconnected from myself. And I had absolutely no clue because I was living just like everyone else around me.

This was what prompted me to share the story of my ten-year journey inward in my first book. Hopefully, it will inspire others to look deeper into their own. In addition to writing, I am also a public speaker on the topic of emotional self-awareness. Seeing others make these realizations is amazing.

Even though this started out by just wanting to lose weight, unpacking all of the hurt, confusion, and false beliefs actually led me right back to my own soul. Releasing all of that repressed negative energy and allowing my subconscious to stand down from the role of safety monitor brought me into a new level of consciousness, which I will continue to pursue.

My life story has now become my life's work. Opening up my mind to new and fresh perspectives alleviated all of the inner turmoil that drove me to overeat. Unburdening my subconscious of repressed pain removed all of the subliminal messaging that had held me back. For the first time, I was able to feel my own value as a human and that value was not at all tied to any accomplishment or source of income. Connecting deeply with myself for the first time evoked a sense of personal power and freedom.

The gratitude I feel for having taken this path is immeasurable. The life I left behind was filled with disconnection at a hurried pace. I cherish every moment of the new one in its place. I had no idea how much joy, peace, freedom, and love one person could experience. It is my hope that those who read this will find these for themselves too.

Vincent Wiggins, EdD

As an educator in higher education that has just experienced a global pandemic, I am concerned about how we continue to support our students, colleagues, friends, and family in this new norm. I have always supported a holistic approach to supporting an individual, and now more than ever, it is vital that we work to make this approach a reality. As a dean in higher education, I have the opportunity to work with faculty and staff to support students' academic success.

One of my current focus areas is looking at relevant education and programming to provide holistic support to students to achieve their academic goals that align with desired career goals. In my roles in management and as an educator, I have developed various training programs and facilitated workshops for students, faculty, and staff. I have presented on pedagogy, andragogy, and technology at professional conferences.

Since completing my doctorate of Education in Curriculum Design at DePaul University, I have always believed in not just focusing on the content; but especially the need of the individuals to allow them to understand themselves and for me to provide a safe support space for them. This passion continues in my research by focusing on students having a better understanding of their self-efficacy which includes becoming more emotionally aware on how to live in a rewarding space (Grow, 1991; Guglielmino, 1978; Hyland & Kranzow, 2011; Knowles, 1975). The passion is also continued in my role as a Conscious Ambassador that seeks to be effective in higher education to continue to support our students, colleagues, friends, and family in this new norm.

Certified Conscious Ambassador. (Hansra Consulting)

Part One

The Indoctrination Loop Of Unawareness.

Three things that keep us from living a mindfully conscious lifestyle: unreleased programming, unresolved trauma, inability to manage ourselves emotionally.

Chapter One

What Is Self-Awareness?

"I am, so I am aware" is a fucking lie.

W e're all adults here so let's start there. Once we set out on a path as adults, it can be very hard to veer away from it. We set our sights, focus our attention towards those goals and often ignore all other signs along the way.

The same can be said of the perspectives and beliefs we carry as we go. Our beliefs about things like religion, politics, world views and society can be so ingrained that we feel no reason to question or challenge them at all. In fact they feel so real that some people even project them onto the world, as if their way of seeing things was the only way that should matter.

At a certain point we think we know what we're doing, or at the very least, we do our best to fake it. All the while, we believe we know ourselves well too, because we have no reason to doubt that we do. Afterall, we've been with ourselves this whole time, we must know who we are right?

The truth is most of us are very out of touch with ourselves internally. We've been trained to be. But, what if we could change that? What if we understood that the most important relationship you have is the one you have with yourself? And if it's not, then who exactly are you giving your power to and why?

Our life's course was charted by our experiences in childhood. That is the time when all of the beliefs and perspectives are formed, generally being molded by how our caregivers saw the world. That is also the time we gain our foundation for what our adult lives will become. Our most important foundational tool is emotional self-awareness. We land somewhere on a spectrum, which greatly depends on the level of those around us as we grew.

So often we jump into life and start focusing externally on other people's needs. We begin to thing that's just how life is. Wrong. That's just what we've been led to believe and are only now slowly opening our eyes to its treachery. This is the exact thought process that has led to burnout, stress, anxiety, depression, disorder, and dysfunction.

Emotional self-awareness is what allows us to see through those old, outdated ideologies. It's the thing that allows us to step out of the daily drama and get a breath of fresh air to regroup and assess our own presence. It's what drives us to care for ourselves in all the necessary ways for a healthy balanced lifestyle without becoming a self-serving ass. Awareness is knowing you need some downtime and allowing for it without an ounce of guilt being associated with that afternoon nap.

As you do the work in part two you will notice a deeper sense of self emerging as you raise your level emotional self-awareness. The idea that we understand ourselves and our emotions has been overwhelmingly mistaken as an innate human characteristic for decades. Being alive does not make a person emotionally self-aware. Knowing you experience emotions does not make you emotionally self-aware. What indicates awareness is having the capacity to accept full responsibility for your own emotions. Which means you need to acknowledge your emotions in the moment and stop ignoring them and thinking they will just pass on their own.

CONSCIOUSNESS IS UNDER THE RUBBLE

Emotions are with us all day, every day. They are unavoidable and they will not leave us alone no matter how much we may attempt to ignore or dismiss them. The more you shove emotions aside the higher the level of anxiety you will experience.

A few indicators of emotional self-awareness are:

- Having the tools to properly understand and manage your own emotions (Identify, process and release).
- The ability to take full responsibility for how you feel at any given time.
- The ability to self-regulate with frequent emotional check-ins throughout the day.
- The ability to make conscious and healthy decisions and choices for yourself.
- Understanding and practicing social emotional competency.

Examples of diminished emotional awareness would be:

- To blame someone else for how you feel.
- To avoid taking responsibility for your actions.
- Reacting in an emotional outburst rather than responding calmly.
- The use of controlling, deceptive, repressive, and manipulative behavior toward others.
- More extreme examples would be unrestrained anger and violence.

If you are like a lot of people, you probably don't give much thought to your emotions at all until something major has forced you to examine your feelings. But we have feelings all the time, feelings that are very personal to each of us, ones that don't want to be ignored. But due to our upbringings many of us have belief systems that tell us:

- Feelings don't matter, they have no value.
- Emotions are to be ignored or buried.
- Feelings are not to be trusted.
- Emotions, especially those considered negative, are to be feared.
- Being emotional makes you vulnerable and weak.

These belief systems often feel like a very real part of who we are because they were created in our childhoods, and we have learned to accept them as very normal parts of who we are.

Feelings are just feelings. They are meant to be simple and can be our best ally once you understand how they work. They are meant to be fleeting, not stuck, trapped, or repressed. But without the proper knowledge needed to navigate them as you go through your day, they go from being our guide to being our sworn enemy. When repressed, emotions become the origin stories for anxiety, disorder, dysfunction, and depression.

Anxiety is a normal human response. It is not, however, a continued state that we are meant to live in. It's normal to be anxious in certain circumstances. Anxiety enters as a feeling when we need to pay attention to the circumstances at hand and navigate them cautiously. When we properly manage our emotions, anxiety is just a heightened sense of a need for awareness in the moment. A moment to take caution.

We are meant to identify the feelings that arise, look deeper into understanding what that feeling is trying to tell us, process its meaning to help us navigate properly, and then release it so we don't drag it along. Anxiety builds when we don't take these steps. Anxiety grows when we come into adulthood with baggage and can't process properly in real time. Anxiety and depression worsen when we don't know what to do or where to turn for the answers.

CONSCIOUSNESS IS UNDER THE RUBBLE

In many cases, these tools have been lost for generations. There had been little to no education on basic emotional understanding in the past generations. In terms of personal healing and expanding consciousness this gap has been largely overlooked as the important assets they are. We need to acknowledge this gap verbally.

Who taught you to understand and navigate your feelings? Understanding how to manage emotions is not innate. Many times, that question will leave a person shocked to realize that no one had. We were left to pick up what we could within our surroundings, based on how those around us navigated themselves emotionally. Most of the subtle childhood trauma we've all experienced was caused by the lack of emotional self-awareness of our caregivers. A lack which has increased with each generation. Thus, generational trauma.

Research has identified the need to understand emotional awareness and how it can impact individual lives (E. Galit Atlas, PhD; Bessel a. van der Kolk, M.D; Annie Wright LMFT). By contributing this new work towards historical research, we hope to amplify the ability for emotional self-awareness and consciousness to raise exponentially.

Without the crucial life skills needed to simply navigate ourselves properly, it is impossible to fully take responsibility for ourselves on an emotional level. IMPOSSIBLE. And without the ability to take emotional responsibility, it's impossible to gain true self-confidence. Without that confidence, we doubt and question ourselves and often stall or get stuck in life.

This is why we blame circumstances outside of ourselves for our anxiety. Anxiety is NOT an external issue. It's internal. The only reason we carry it around is, through no fault of our own, is because we are missing the tools to manage it.

This has created what we call the indoctrination loop of unawareness. This loop has been perpetrated by the prolonged encouragement to ignore ourselves internally and seek outwardly instead.

This loop pushes us to repeat dysfunctional behavior. It makes it difficult to control our anger and fear. It's why we continually repeat the same fights in our relationships or subliminally seek out the same type of partners.

This loop creates a constant internal conflict between the false ego-self that believes we know what we are doing (seeing/portraying ourselves as confident, strong, and in control) and the very authenticity of our soul which seeks truth, peace, love, and happiness.

That conflict increases anxiety and keeps us hidden from our own truth. We feel shame when none of this has ever been our fault. So let yourself off the hook for what you didn't know in the past and realize that it's up to you to now learn a better path forward. Why? Because they will change your life and together we will change the world.

Author's notes: Every little Penny counts.

You may consider yourself an emotional person. You may realize when you are sad or angry. I thought of myself as a very emotional person. I cried, got angry, etc. What I didn't do was actually connect with myself emotionally because I'd been taught to push my feelings aside in my youth rather than acknowledge them and learn what they meant.

It wasn't until I went through this 10-year journey that I began to sit down and acknowledge that being aware that I had emotions didn't mean I was emotionally self-aware. Emotional self-awareness means you know better than to dismiss or ignore your emotions. Instead, you acknowledge them and pay attention to what they are telling you.

Feelings are meant to be fleeting, but fleeting doesn't mean they are to be dismissed. Feelings happen to alert us to the potential effects of our surroundings. They tell us how much we can trust the people and situations around us. They point us back to things we don't like about ourselves or are insecure about. And, when left unattended they cause a buildup of anxiety and leave us blocked from some of the things we most desire. It's easy to think that everyone gets angry when driving in traffic.

It's easy to believe the way the majority of us have become is just normal because so many of us are the same when it comes to how we view emotions. I know it can be hard to see a reason to look deeper because I did the same. I didn't look deeper for the first 53 years of my life. I only did so because I had to, but it has such a profound effect on my life I have devoted my time to talking about the importance.

The difference in living like it is normal and continuing to be angry at other drivers and asking yourself what it was specifically about something a particular driver did that upset you is like night and day once you've experienced it. As we go through our day and someone ticks us off, those moments are showing us something inside us that needs to be examined or healed. For example, if a driver cuts you off ask yourself what exactly came up in those moments. Was it a fear that you'd be injured? Was it the pain of being minimized because it seemed that they took something from you by moving into what you considered your personal space? Did you feel taken advantage of because they got ahead of you and now you feel you have to "show them"?

I used to get so upset when someone got into my space in traffic. I realized it caused a feeling of being minimized. As I began to tie that to my past I found ample examples of that in my childhood. My anger was not at the driver, it was because of my past unprocessed pain. Working the actual problem removed all that for me. The way other people drive is no longer a personal experience for me. I recognize everyone has their own stuff and reasons for their behavior which has nothing to do with me personally.

CONSCIOUSNESS IS UNDER THE RUBBLE

Once you truly look deeper into emotions instead of just swatting them away, they hold immense value and insight into you and how you became how you are. This is why facing those moments as much as possible can free you from a buildup of anxiety, because you actually navigate them and not kick the to the curb!

You might be saying to yourself, who has time for all that right? Well, take a look at how much time and money you end up spending avoiding your emotions. Be honest about your retail therapy and comfort food or other avoidant coping you use. Those are costly distractions and repressed emotions are driving them. We all add so much chaos to our lives, simply by not facing inward enough.

When you do that, when you don't value how you feel it contributes to feelings of having less personal value internally. You won't notice it because it's been part of your programming as a youth, and it seemed normal as almost everyone is doing it these days! But that programming created a belief that how you felt had no value, which leads to the loop of ignoring how you feel and continues the feeling of having no/less value. Which continues any current issues or fears you are facing as well as avoidance.

Once you become more in tune with yourself emotionally it will be much easier to see the childhood connections. You will be able to relate current feelings back to ones you have felt in the past and find core root issues that cause current insecurity or blocks.

It's then you can go back and think about your childhood and think of who showed you how to be this way, to have these beliefs by asking what/who the example was? Was it your mom doing the same thing? Was it your rank in the family that put you in that position? Was it something your second-grade teacher said to you?

For example, if you carry the fear that someone won't like you and don't understand why, you can't release yourself from the fear so you will proceed in the same manner in real time today.

In truth there will be people who don't like you and it will have zero to do with you. We all trigger pain points in each other. We all have lessons we bring to others so they can learn and grow too. But they won't like us for that if they want to remain stuck and in denial. If this makes sense, then it will start to make sense why catching our feelings as they happen are such great guides to our own success, etc.

Chapter Two

The Big Disconnect.

If we were taught to see emotions as the GPS through life that they actually are we would not fear them and would feel much safer in all situations.

To unleash our true inner power and reconnect with our souls, you will see in part two that we must look in two directions, back and inward. The past holds the key, and we hold the answers. When we begin to trust ourselves to find those answers, (instead of looking outside ourselves) we build internal trust and open the door to freedom.

Many times, people hold a fear that they will re-live the pain if they review past experiences. That fear comes from two places. One is the confusion we've encountered by not having proper understanding of emotions. The second is not realizing we will be viewing it as an adult, not a vulnerable and dependent child. As adults, we can view the pain the child endured, release it and process the events with the understanding of an adult. Understanding dysfunctional patterns and their origins is the key to unlocking unwanted behavior.

Let's start by looking further into how the lack of proper guidance has affected our lives. Without the ability to take responsibility for ourselves emotionally we have given our own personal power away in a myriad of ways that include:

- We can't explain why we feel anxious.
- We blame people for how they "make" us feel.
- We don't assess our feelings properly during the day.
- We disassociate from ourselves and our bodies.
- We use distraction and avoidance as coping.
- We can't form deep, strong connections with others.
- We have difficulty being emotionally available and present in relationships, including those with our own children.
- We mistake emotions distance and the inability to properly cope as disorders and mental illness.
- We seek external validation or remedy.
- Lacking the foundational elements, which are necessary for our own emotional well-being, leaves us at a disadvantage in all aspects of life. Not only are we unable to properly cope in real time, but we are also unable to dislodge and release repressed emotions as well.

In order for us to have grown into well-balanced, mindful human beings, the childhood years needed to have progressed us with the basics: proper emotional guidance with appropriate levels of knowledge at appropriate ages and times.

When that doesn't happen...enter the subconscious. The subconscious is the culprit that gets involved and runs in the background, preventing us from being fully mindful, conscious and present in all of our decisions making and choices. It does this for one reason only - it thinks it is protecting us.

The role of the subconscious in our childhood development is enormous. It's the gatekeeper of our well-being. It determines our entire future based on what it's seen over the course of our childhood and will, unfortunately, continue as such into our adult lives if we have not been trained to properly manage emotions, fully cope, and consciously assume responsibility. It has been monitoring our experiences, constantly scanning everything from the purview of our personal and emotional safety. The culmination of all these experiences combine to form a set of constructs causing the subconscious to:

Accept the role of emotional safety monitor.

Determine our perspectives about what social belief systems we will follow.

Take all of the messaging we have received about how others view us and create personal beliefs about who we are including our internal value, worth, esteem, and place within this world and establish a false outer persona.

These things determine how we behave, who we become, and where we get stuck. The subconscious was buzzing around in the background of our lives creating our future, our false persona, and our personality.

We were not born into any of it. We were molded based on what was happening around us. But the good news is that none of this is fixed, including our personalities. The belief that people can't change is false. People can change with the proper knowledge and determination. Once we further understand what childhood and the subconscious created for us, we can work to change it. And then finally create what it is we really do want.

Unless you have had very conscious, accepting, openminded, and emotionally intelligent parents or mentors who encouraged you to experiment, chances are your beliefs and perspectives have not been shaped by your own conscious choices.

Children are completely trusting in the vulnerability of those early years and fully depend on others for their very survival. Learning to accept what is being taught and modeled as normal becomes a natural part of growing up. The idea of questioning anything from the childhood years may never arise.

CONSCIOUSNESS IS UNDER THE RUBBLE

This is how the subconscious began to direct the continuous unwanted behavior we've been wanting to ditch for decades. This is where addictions begin. This is where are traits, both good and bad begin. This is where are relationship patterns are fostered.

This really isn't the role the subconscious is supposed to have in our lives. It's supposed to manage all of the multiple actions we take on at once, like walking and chewing gum at the same time. But due to the lack of training, guidance, and proper examples of emotional self-awareness, the subconscious has had to take on a much broader role for us. The role of emotional protector.

Hidden and unprocessed pain, fear, and confusion drive triggered and unwanted behavior. The subconscious monitors our ability to manage ourselves emotionally at each age. It keeps track of all situations in which pain, fear, or confusion are left unprocessed. Those are referenced as painful pressure points. They are red flagged as trigger points where the subconscious believes it will need to step in as protection when alerted. This causes the subconscious to stay in a state of readiness, which creates a continued state of low-level anxiety (finding, processing, and releasing the repressed energies removes the anxiety). This is happening all through our childhood. The building of our internal sentry.

This was the origin of most, if not all avoidant coping strategies. The mind and body have trapped and repressed energy that needs soothing (and releasing). Once the pain points are triggered the subconscious sweeps away our ability to proceed consciously as it seeks methods of soothing. This is why addiction and other dysfunctional behaviors seem so impossible to break, because the underlying hidden trigger points has not been released. Until that has been accomplished, the behavior will remain.

These deeply hidden and unresolved emotions (when triggered) that drive our insecurities will also obviously have a large impact on our social interactions. Because we've not been fully and properly trained to manage our emotions, we then naturally feel exposed and vulnerable in social settings.

The lack of awareness of our past pain points and inability to manage our emotions in real time create a shaky emotional foundation and will naturally create feelings of apprehension and defensiveness.

In this state we are more likely to become judgmental and critical of others. We do this as we compare ourselves to those around us (out of doubt and insecurity) which will result in making ourselves feel better or worse at any given time. These moments, where we are less accepting of ourselves also cause increased anxiety.

The good news is, at the same time, the soul uses the dysfunction to call our attention to that old unprocessed pain. Because on a conscious level our actions are self-defeating, making us want to rid ourselves of the behavior.

This is why we feel so much guilt and shame when we keep repeating unwanted behaviors. Our soul is seeking a return to our truths. That old, painful energy wants to be cleared. So, when we say we just want it to go away, that's what our soul wants too.

Once we learn to look inward we can learn to use these breadcrumbs to find the original pain points and release them. Thus, freeing ourselves from the trigger points one at a time. At the same time, the subconscious has been monitoring our ability to relate to the outside world. It will seek to recreate or replicate situations similar to those unresolved from our past when it comes to the partners we choose. Because it's looking to have those resolved. It's been well researched similar to the finding by Dr. Atlas that unresolved issues with parents are often mirrored not only with our romantic partners but in many other aspects of our lives.

"Emotional Inheritance is about silenced experiences that belong not only to us but to our parents, grandparents, and great-grandparents, and about the ways they impact our lives. It is these secrets that often keep us from living to our full potential. They affect our mental and physical health, create gaps between what we want for yourselves and what we are able to have, and haunt us like ghosts."

(Galit Atlas, PhD; 2022)

Emotional Inheritance: A Therapist, Her Patients, and the Legacy of Trauma.

False and limiting beliefs cause insecurity. We all have conditioned beliefs we've let slide like they are a living breathing part of who we are. We have even learned to believe they are part of our personality and that they are "fixed."

Often, we will even confuse these beliefs with facts, rather than simply the personal things we choose to believe. These sneaky bastards started showing up as a result of various messaging and patterns recognized by the subconscious that were modeled to us when we were kids.

Almost all of what we do is a result of how our brains process each of our experiences, and depending on the positive or negative effects, we may either mirror or reject specific behavior patterns.

Again, there are large portions of the way we live the lives that we did not consciously choose. This happens when a caregiver has subtly projected some or many of their personal perspectives, expectations, and beliefs. How they see themselves, us as their offspring, other relationships, work, education, popularity, and life are projected via their actions and messaging. That messaging is what conditions and shapes our own belief systems. Generations of unresolved fears and insecurities have influenced our belief systems and will continue to do so until we choose to examine them more closely.

For example, if your mother took on the role of caregiver to many people, you may carry a strong feeling of responsibility for everyone in your inner circle. Or if she was an exercise junkie, you may become a Navy Seal. Both are true stories (based on one of the author's personal experiences).

Then there are the less positive experiences: if your mother was treated as if she didn't exist, she may treat you similarly. And while it will feel like a deeply painful personal attack, it was not directed at you personally. Anyone could have been in your place and received the same abusive treatment.

With this new research on the effects of generational trauma and conditioning, we no longer have to rely upon existing outdated assumptions.

It's just as likely not in your bloodline, it is very possible that it doesn't have as much to do with genetics or DNA as we've been led to believe. In fact, it is becoming clear that it has more to do with survival than anything else.

The brain of a child will create a safety zone which will be considered normal for that child based upon their experiences and often there is no reason to question it as anything less than reality.

Messaging comes in many formats and is often very subtle. They can feel very personal to us when they are about:

- Our appearance.
- Our choices.
- Our grades.
- Our emotions.
- How we fit in.
- The amount of attention placed on other family members.
- Or any number of things that can be internalized depending on circumstances.

But again, remember, anyone having that experience could have had the same treatment because it originates from the perspectives of the parent and any unresolved issues they have.

The more consistent the messaging is and the more confidently it is modeled by the caregiver, the more we learn to believe it and the more it seems real. And the stronger the internal insecurity will become when left unaddressed. The overall tone in which parents present themselves and the way discipline is managed reinforces the need the subconscious has in creating a safety zone.

It doesn't matter how subtle or well-intended, if what is presented feels like an attack directed toward the individual rather than a correction of their actions, the emotion in those moments will leave a mark. Often those moments will create or build upon any existing false beliefs.

This will directly affect how we feel about ourselves, who we are and how we see our own value. It will affect both self-care and how we care for and about others. But, in each moment, we will be left unaware of what we are building. And every single child has been put at a disadvantage like this in some way because every parent carries forward some baggage from their own childhood years.

Conditioned beliefs of others are absorbed as truths. Other types of messaging serve to determine how we understand our place in society. Although there are many other contributing factors such as environment, income level, extended family, and so on, our own emotional self-awareness significantly contributes to this.

Parents with higher levels of self-awareness and emotional intelligence will naturally project more kindness and compassion. This fosters healthier beliefs about ourselves, others, and our place in the world. These messages create a more positive feeling of trust and safety in ourselves, others, the world, and life in general. Those feelings of safety allow us to manage ourselves from a more consciously aware and solid foundation.

A strong emotional foundation gives us more command of how we navigate our way thought life. It cuts out the need for external control and validation.

Whereas families who experience lower levels of emotional self-awareness will carry higher levels of unexamined fear, pain, and insecurities. They will encourage feelings to be ignored because they are misunderstood or seen to have no value.

These parents often project the unexamined insecurities along with distrust and doubt and will clearly leave the child feeling far less safe in the world. These types of generational insecurities and conditioning can often result in deeply hidden anxieties that can cause the subconscious to form a larger-than-life false persona to compensate for the lack they feel. A few traits are:

- Continually seeking validation externally.
- A desperate need for control and power.
- A self-serving, disregard for others.
- A sense of entitlement.
- A false belief of superiority which is often accompanied by hatred.
- An unhealthy relationship with money tied to greed.

Authoritarian false beliefs, thinking what one believes personally is what's best for the world.

The pain can be very deeply hidden. The conditioning may have been so intensely presented as absolute truths that these individuals often become fully invested in both false beliefs and their own false personas.

They will defend them at all costs. Even the destruction of others, even that of all humanity. The more power the subconscious uses to seek safety the more unconscionable behaviors are acceptable to those who find themselves in these unfortunate circumstances. They can either become masters at manipulation and seem to have a commanding presence or become vulnerable to those who seem commanding. History is filled with examples of the horrors brought on by the lack of emotional awareness and intelligence.

Author's notes: A bad Penny always turns up. The feelings I had were deep, but they were also buried very deeply. I used everything I had, each moment when I questioned what was happening I took it back to the core. When I felt rushed at the gas station and no one else was around, I found a belief that I was always in the way. When certain friendships seemed one-sided, I found the root of being unwanted. I left nothing as an innate trait, I questioned it all. Which was how I finally made peace with myself.

Chapter Three

Life By Default.

To protect and sooth.

The subconscious gets so good at doing its secondary job of soothing and protecting, we are easily often unaware how much of our lives are lived by default. We can have no idea of our own lack of conscious choice or consent. This makes understanding the subconscious vital, because this lack of understanding is what keeps us in direct conflict with ourselves.

The subconscious and the conscious have two different forms of logic. When we seek to resolve things within the logic of our conscious brain and ignore the subconscious, we will continue to loop and live by default.

While it may be more natural to consciously desire solutions which are logical and healthy, when triggered, our subconscious reacts in fear and panic. It's simply seeking to soothe and reestablish safety. Because without the necessary training on emotional management, the only choice the subconscious sees is to drive our behavior toward the dysfunctional solutions of avoidant coping.

The repressed and unaddressed issues our subconscious holds will override all logic in its attempt to protect and soothe us in those moments of panic. Remember, the subconscious is operating from a deep history of terror and lack in these specific moments. And without doing the work to locate and dislodge those pain points which are being triggered we have no hope of releasing the subconscious override. Addiction is not incurable. No one has figured out how to cure it until now.

Imagine if the healthiest choices were easy all of the time. Imagine never overeating when you are full or never drinking more than you intended. Imagine if the desire to exercise was at the top of your mind and the things we enjoyed were all of the things that were truly the best for ourselves. Almost no one lives this way. But it's absolutely possible, once we engage the subconscious and help it release its need to control us out of fear, by processing the unresolved fear and learning emotional management. And it's also your choice how much of the work you do at a time.

In order to put ourselves consciously back in charge of all of our choices, we must become very aware of the patterns within our behaviors and learn to identify and understand their origins. Those false beliefs that were created during the indoctrination period from messaging, whether subtle or obvious, have markers we can find based on our insecurities and behavior patterns.

In part two we will explore that further but first; we have to allow ourselves to understand that those beliefs are not truths. They are not a fixed part of our personalities. They are only what make up the false persona that keeps us safe in the eye of the subconscious, and also what keeps us small, and our souls hidden.

The more we have learned to hide our feelings and the more doubt we feel about ourselves, the more the innocence of our soul is overshadowed by that false persona. Over time we learned to build up a hardened outer shell of the false self as the tenderest parts of ourselves retreat. We learn to fear vulnerability, which will hinder our ability to form strong connections. If we can't feel safe to be vulnerable with ourselves, we will absolutely not feel safe with anyone else. If we left childhood unknowing feeling unsafe, we would live in fear.

CONSCIOUSNESS IS UNDER THE RUBBLE

Most of us enter into our adult lives in that default mode and live by the terms of our indoctrination. Without a safe, solid internal foundation we become fixated on external means of security and focus on financial independence. Because we do not feel secure or safe with ourselves. So, we let that false personal forge ahead with a faulty set of priorities. And because the subconscious is both the curator and the guard we remain unaware. We loop in default.

The more financially successful we believe ourselves to be, the less interested we become in anything outside of that perception. However, the more we stay in pursuit of finance the more we depend on money for happiness. The more we work, the less happy we become, and the more anxiety builds. The more anxiety we feel, the more we seek distraction from the outside world. The more we anchor ourselves externally the less inner peace and personal power we have. Humanity may have reached the breaking point when it comes to this type of lifestyle, as more people are beginning to seek out a better work-life balance. Emotional self-awareness is the key to finding sustainable balance and inner peace.

While you may be making many conscious choices about your life and your future, they are likely based on past indoctrination which means the subconscious is directing you a massive amount of the time. This is why some people hit the ground running and some stall. This is why people from the same households turn out so differently. This is why you may feel very confident in some areas but terrified in others.

What we consider the comfort zone is the subconscious safety mode. This is also why it's said we learn the most once we get outside of our comfort zone. Because stepping out of our comfort zone is exactly when we begin to step out of the default safety mode of the subconscious. It's here where we can become more consciously aware and start to seek ways out of the loop of indoctrination and where we can start to engage with ourselves more fully and wholly.

Personal growth is a process. It won't happen overnight. It won't happen if you ignore any of the steps because the subconscious will continually pull you back into the safety of the comfort zone if you do. This is why addiction has been labeled as a disease in the past and has been treated like a mental disorder before research was done on the effects of childhood on adult behavior patterns.

We will see that the subconscious holds the answers for nearly all dysfunction and disorder. Along with all of our blocks and fears. We will see that the inability to self-monitor and regulate our emotions holds the answer to most of our blocks. However, until that is explored on a personal level, our default mode will remain fully intact and in charge of our actions, no matter how hard we fight against it. And the stronger the false persona of egotistical beliefs, the less likely you will engage in personal growth.

When we see people taking unconscionable actions against humanity, they are working in the default mode within the indoctrination loop of unawareness. The less internal power a person feels, the more likely they are to seek it externally. The more likely they are to support or align with those who they perceive to enable them in that search. If you don't understand what drives greed, the need to possess massive firearms or be authoritarian and controlling of others it all circles back to a deep feeling of being internally powerless and lacking emotional self-awareness.

We are not born into this loop. We inherit parts of it and collect the rest along the way. Parenting is a messy job and often the only training we have gotten was in watching our own parents. In cultures that do not understand the importance of the childhood years or hold enough reverence for the job of parenting, we are exposed to a multitude of problems.

Unaware parents will not be as emotionally available to their children or be capable of understanding or accepting of their child's emotional needs. Children will likely be taught to fit in rather than encouraged to explore who they'd like to become. If parents lack empathy they will subliminally encourage the emotional shut down of their children by not letting their emotions be expressed or understood.

CONSCIOUSNESS IS UNDER THE RUBBLE

It's very possible to have stronger and deeper connections with our families. It's possible to do the repair work to heal together. We may need to let go of a few false beliefs. While it is true that most parents do their very best for their children, it's clear that we've all been missing out on some very basic fundamental understanding for generations.

And while our caregivers did their best, that doesn't diminish or dismiss how we were left feeling. We have no one to blame but the continuation of what has been. As parents, if we allow for the fact that if we had received better training we could have done better, we can then begin to accept that our children have experienced really painful, traumatic, and confusing situations that were not addressed properly. That pain needs to not only be healed but acknowledged and validated as real.

Simply doing our best was all that was possible at that time, of course. But that cannot continue to be an excuse for the results our children experience because by doing that, we continue to minimize the emotional experiences of their childhoods. When we don't have the ability to openly talk about this within our relationships it becomes the pain our children silently wear across their hearts. And, if heavy enough, it becomes the burdens they silently carry on their backs. This is the very heart of generational trauma.

We have all been indoctrinated. It carries on from one generation to the next in our families, in society, and in schools. Adapting to or rebelling against the beliefs of those around us will set the tone for who we become. We've silently agreed, often giving it no thought or awareness. Any type of trauma keeps us anchored to the past until it is released.

Children who have been discouraged to share their emotions, especially within their own families, become at risk. While parents may understand that a screaming child is truly okay, the child doesn't feel okay and doesn't understand why the parent can't see that. Especially if they pain was not acknowledged and validated initially. When a child's questions are frequently pushed aside by busy parents, it sends a message to that child that both their emotions as well as they themselves are seen as unimportant. Having little or no means to navigate the experiences successfully will create discomfort and cause internal disconnect as well as possible disassociation from our own bodies. Because safety is the subconscious' focus, no matter what it takes, even the most egregious self-defeating behaviors.

Just as in childhood, as we go on with our lives, the feelings that need to be consciously processed and released throughout the day get pushed aside, because we've learned that is a normal behavior. The real-time unprocessed emotions cause anxiety which compounds the anxiety we feel from the repressed emotions of our childhood experiences. Anxiety keeps shifting us into a survival-mode frame of mind as the subconscious seeks to comfort us. As if we are signaling an S.O.S. since we are living in survival override syndrome.

This has gone on so long that we no longer recognize anxiety as a natural process of the human experience. We have learned to fear anxiety, labeling it as a disorder when it may very often be the product of an inability to navigate our emotions properly. Think about this. It's not about the loss of a job that makes us anxious, it's the fear we have around the change that loss will create and what that loss says about us. It's about how you feel about that fear and the steps we fail to take to navigate that emotional fear that results in the buildup of anxiety. Unprocessed emotions are energy. Even though you may go out and find a new job quickly, that unprocessed energy remains and will have a powerful hold on you until resolved.

Author's Notes: The Penny Lane of old

When I picture the first fifty plus years of my life it seems very heavy, like I was slogging my way though, tromping heavily as I went. It was like a whirlwind of trying to stay ahead of the game or trying to stay on top of everything with no end in sight.

CONSCIOUSNESS IS UNDER THE RUBBLE

I thought I was living a life I had chosen. But I hadn't purposely picked any of the things I did. I wanted another life for myself but allowed this one to happen instead. There are times when I understand that had I not done that time I wouldn't have been able to dedicate a decade to research and my own introspection.

But the more I moved out of the grind the more I saw a totally different way of looking at life. The way things have always been done, or the way they used to be doesn't have to be how we do it any longer. The problem is, when you've been programmed to believe that is the way life is, like I had been and when you fall into adulting by default without knowing how to question anything, it's entirely possible and far too easy to stay in default.

I fully believed I was aware, because I had no idea this other way of life even existed. But every time I found the reason for a piece of anxiety and questioned the situation that caused it, the doorway opened up a bit more. It was like knocking bricks out of the path to my happy place.

I started learning about my own false beliefs. In the back of my mind, I felt I had no value. I felt I was in the way. I felt like I needed a layer of padding for protection and a scowl on my face to keep anyone from questioning me. I tied back the value issue to being told no by my parents to pretty much everything I wanted as a kid. I started to notice people in my life as an adult who also minimized me. And I started to want no part of that any longer.

Personal work like this is very personal and it's all about you and not what anyone else thinks. I am still in the process of losing weight. In some ways it's become a bit less urgent, but it's something I want and will still do. For a while, I held back on sharing my story because I thought I had to be at my goal weight to be believable and that's not true. All of the things I've been through can help others now. Holding it in out of pride and vanity is silly. If someone wants to judge me, that's on them and their issues. Not me.

Chapter Four

An Open-Minded Pursuit Of The Truth.

Conscious traits like kindness and empathy can be hidden behind pain and insecurity.

Admittedly, self-reflection can unearth some surprises. Learning that the connection between our caregivers, childhood and the present are so deeply entwined can be jarring. And it's a strange place to find yourself when you finally admit all of the choices of your life may not have been what you really wanted.

The ways learned in child become hard wired, almost baked in, especially beliefs. Our belief systems are responsible for how we live our lives. Which makes it that much more important to realize that beliefs are not actual truths. Perspectives are not truths. Perceptions are not truths. Opinions are not truths. Truth is based facts, not personal viewpoints.

Beliefs, when driven by insecurity and fear, pit us against ourselves and each other, because they become self- serving in nature and go against the betterment of all mankind. Beliefs can also be false in nature. When we continually hear things that demean us as children we will begin to think negatively about ourselves.

CONSCIOUSNESS IS UNDER THE RUBBLE

This is why it can be so important to examine false beliefs (as we will in part two) that we may have around what certain types of relationships mean. For the older generations, many of us were raised by media falsely portraying relationships as supportive (Father knows best) when those in our lives were not. We can spend massive amounts of energy in harmful relationships because of the beliefs those messages created. It's important that we allow ourselves to release those false beliefs and stop pretending the people around us (caregivers) were not just flawed humans. And also recognizing that some of the people we are in other relationships with mirror our caregivers.

Another belief we are now seeing is false is the labeling of disorders caused by emotional distress as mental illness.

The lack of emotional well-being should not constitute a mental illness when a lack of proper guidance and tools are what have caused it. There is a very real and significant difference between psychological damage and emotional distress.

It's very likely that many medications will become unnecessary as a deeper understanding and more training become mainstream in education. And when the time to process and release old wounds is a natural path towards healing.

In the past the need to find solutions became more important than looking for the reason the solutions were needed. And emotional dysfunction drives a massive amount of consumerism. In worst-case scenarios, humanity is being devoured by the insecurity-driven behaviors of the emotionally repressed via conditioned hatred. In the best case, we are finally embracing the traumas of childhood and looking to teach the next generations properly. We still have billions who have been left in the dark.

As we look inward and reflect we will see that past indoctrination has paved the way for not only programming and false beliefs but assumptions as well. The default mode we enter adulthood in is filled with false assumptions that many things are innate, which are not.

By now we see that understanding our own emotions was not innate, meaning that emotional self-awareness is also not innate. As far back as 1999, author Carolyn Saarni believed that emotional abilities were not innate, but instead cultivated and developed through children's interactions with others. She defined emotions as a component of self-efficacy.

The false assumptions we have continued to live by have created other gaps in understanding as well. By arbitrarily thinking we "are" so we know ourselves well, we then tend to think that self-care, self-love, and self- acceptance are all innately understood. When many times that has been turned into a commercially high- maintenance process.

These are things that need to originate internally rather than being driven by a need for external gratification. For example:

Focusing on your job more than your health is the opposite of self-care.

Allowing abuse in your relationships is the opposite of self-love.

Seeing yourself as pretty only when wearing makeup is the opposite of self-acceptance.

For so long we've been fully accepting of the way things are because we didn't know the importance of questioning how they became that way. As our souls retreated during indoctrination, our subconscious closed down our emotions and walled us off out of fear of continued unmanageable pain. At the same time, many of us lost touch with ourselves not only emotionally but physically and spiritually, which connect us with our own humanity.

Another thing that is not innate is empathy and without empathy we also lose the ability to have compassion and offer kindness. Especially toward those we see through lenses of comparison or judgment. Without empathy we become disconnected, both internally and externally.

For example, those who practice self-serving and egregiously authoritarian behavior, those who insist their beliefs to be real truths or even believe lies as truths have lost their ability to connect with humanity. Often they believe themselves to be highly connected because of religious beliefs. Again, this becomes the case during the childhood experience. It's not necessary to judge people in these extreme situations. It's more important to understand their stories that created those behaviors. Otherwise, more negativity and conflict will be created.

Again, the key to disarming these destructive human traits will also be in understanding how they came to be, which will generally go straight back to childhood and societal conditioning. Hatred and superiority is taught by adults. If we look closer we will likely see those who are immersed in the fear of losing control. Control is what they have learned to believe is their only means of having power. If they are not self-aware or reflective, they won't realize that if they dismantled their own painful fear- based insecurity they could reclaim their own personal power. Lack of acceptance, judgement and hatred drives destruction and most of this is drawn from religious books written by human beings. If we each had the ability to manage our own emotions and remain calm, we could more deeply examine these divides without harming others. Emotional self-awareness allows us to look more fully at the big picture of all situations rather than have a need to home in on finding specific details to substantiate our own personal beliefs.

There are also many other types outdated beliefs about the importance of the childhood years. Most of which create a narrow one-sided journey that minimizes and marginalizes the adult lives of many children. A few examples would be:

Kids can't know what's best for themselves.

All children are extremely resilient.

CONSCIOUSNESS IS UNDER THE RUBBLE

Children don't remember those early years.

Caregivers with lower levels of emotional self-awareness unintentionally limit the future decision-making of their children in many ways. A one-sided conversation in the form of a lecture rather than the open communication of proper guidance leaves little room for a child to understand or explore their own truths.

When the personal belief systems of the parents or their culture are projected as undeniable truths it also leaves no room for choice for the individual child. Vulnerable children will have no choice but to accept "this is the way things are done" and believe it must be the real truth. They will learn to look no further, carrying the beliefs forward that "knowing" they are right in what they are doing without question. These types of childhood situations are what propagate narrow- minded, inflexible, and authoritarian thought processes. Along with senseless destruction and murder.

The more fearful we are to show vulnerability, the more we will want to hide all things connected to our emotions. We now have dueling identities. Our soul wants to be seen, live freely, and be safe doing so. Our subconsciously created persona, however, wants to avoid most things beneath the surface level.

Neither side has balance. As the created persona tries to keep the soul at bay it wants to defy anything that could be perceived as weakness. If you can't connect inwardly you will likely not care about the effect you have on others because you will be too busy defending yourself. And, it's likely that you felt uncared about in some important ways as a child.

Showing empathy toward another is impossible if you are disconnected from your own emotions. You lack the emotional connection internally to imagine what another person is going through because you would not be emotionally affected by it yourself. You would blow it off or shrug it off like it didn't matter, so, why, in your mind should it matter to you on behalf of another. It should be noted here that people who have become manipulative have become good at reading others' emotions, which can be mistaken as empathy. When in reality they only use the information for manipulative purposes while portraying themselves as empathic and caring humans.

To further understand how people become self-serving, we must be aware that people who feel powerless internally and have been conditioned in hatred can be vulnerable to those who appear to make them feel powerful. They not only disconnect from their own integrity but will defend and excuse those who lack integrity as well. The same could be said of those conditioned to believe themselves superior which will often render their focus on their particular needs, deeming the needs of others irrelevant.

Insecure messaging in childhood often leads children to believe that needing emotional support or love, or feeling emotions means we are weak individuals. This is why we fear vulnerability. This is why we live in pain and disorder. We are afraid of being seen as weak. We are afraid of being seen at all because the best of ourselves is still hidden. We've gradually built up and accepted a certain hopelessness about ourselves.

Parents are not always capable of keeping their children emotionally safe, because of their own upbringing. With each generation, remnants of trauma, large and small, are passed down to the next. Everything left unexplained compounds the effects of the trauma. Wars, economic constraints, hate crimes, and discrimination impact the citizens involved and their descendants at length. Each insecurity caused by the confusion and inability to properly manage the emotions that was brought on by circumstances festers, shaping beliefs and perceptions which are then projected down through the generations.

Until you take time to find a safe way to unpack and unload all that you've been carrying, you cannot be free. Read that again. And this means to fully unload. You have to get in there just as you would if you wanted to detail your own car. No surface wipe downs. Not just cleaning the floor mats. Clean the carpet underneath too. Get in there and find that old piece of food that's been stinking up the place and rid yourself of it.

This is why it is so important to create a safe space. The safer you feel, the more comfortable you will be with vulnerability. The more fearful you are the more defensive you will become. The degree of kindness you received at home, the more it seemed that you mattered, the more it seemed everyone mattered, is what set the stage for where you fall on the spectrum of emotional self-awareness. Everyone has things they will benefit by unpacking their own emotional baggage. Because everyone has some type of baggage.

Author's Notes: A Penny for your thoughts.

In the past ten years there hasn't been one issue or one conversation about someone else's issue that has not led back to an experience from those childhood years. Everyone we encounter can have a lasting effect on us in those years. But it's hard to notice or pay attention to how affected we are if we had been told to ignore how things have made us feel.

Imagine what it feels like in times when you feel overwhelmed as an adult now. Then think back about what it must have been like for us as children. When we have too much happening at once or too much confusion, things can become very difficult to navigate. As a child, who was meant to be a feeling human with normal emotions, without being given any way to understand or manage those feelings and especially if there has been messaging that emotions are meaningless and should be ignored, we probably felt buried in confusion. For the purposes of this work, do not ignore any the possibility that any of your current actions are likely tied back to those years.

Chapter Five

Living Within The Flow Of Life.

Reflection is the door to the soul.

The most important relationship we each have is the one we have with ourselves, especially that with our conscious selves, which is the most connected to our soul. That starts with the open-minded willingness to become emotionally responsible and self-aware. It continues by doing the work to remove the subconscious blocks which will allow us to connect to ourselves most deeply, and more deeply with others.

Many of us were taught to mistrust ourselves because we were raised by people who distrusted themselves, and that's okay. There is no one to blame here. The need to blame is just a product of deflection and denial. Change is not found in denial. Again, change is found in understanding why you do what you do - at the source.

The benefits of increased personal self-awareness and emotional intelligence are undeniable, and you will begin to see this in part two. When we open our minds to things outside the scope of our original indoctrination, our lives can unfold in some very different and amazing ways.

Uprooting the foothold that the subconscious held in our lives clears our path to a conscious and mindful lifestyle. Removing each of the varying types of blockages that obstructed our energy which caused the flow of life to move around us now allows for life to flow through us instead. Joy, freedom, happiness, and inner peace exist within that flow, our desired lifestyles flow toward us. We are then free to exist in a peaceful state of acceptance, so solid within we no longer feel the need to seek outwardly.

A state of increased flow will also:

Cause appropriate people, things, and situations to flow into life without effort.

Allow our instincts to keep us safe so there is no longer a need for defensiveness. Increase internal acceptance, freeing us from the need to compare ourselves to others. Increase acceptance of others, freeing us from the need to judge others or ourselves.

Help us recognize that our happiness should NOT come at the expense of others.

Relax the insecurity-based need for external control.

Remove the need for authorism behavior and allow everyone to make their own choices without forcing our choices and beliefs on others.

Remove the conditioned fears that drive hatred and a false sense of supremacy.

Allows for the ability to accept each person where they are on their own journey because we lose the harmful projections of "you should be happy" or "you always have a choice" based on how we see their experiences.

Expectations of others as well as expectations of certain outcomes often block the flow within us. As we become more aware we are able to see how little we feel the need to control outcome or try and change those around us. When those aspects are removed all things become less personal which removes the judgment and criticism and allows for more observation. (Chapter 12, Reflection Key Points can also be used while observing others).

When we have moved into a higher state of consciousness in our own lives we can begin to recognize how the conditioned and fear-charged beliefs cause all of the unconscionable behavior in humanity. Insecurity keeps humanity blocked off from their own soul. Such a hardened form of indoctrination and such deep layers of insecurity and fear makes it much harder for the soul to emerge from behind the false persona.

When we position ourselves more in a place of personal power we find far more acceptance for ourselves, others, and the world. As our soul emerges from beneath the rubble we can stand taller within that power. We regain our voice and are free to help others as they begin to emerge themselves. Within our relationships it is important to understand our impact. While we may all be doing our best, it does not give us the right to minimize the pain someone feels when interacting with us. Especially, if they are not in a position to accept full responsibility for their own emotions. Positioning ourselves with a better foundation will provide more understanding toward preventing this in the future.

Author's notes: A Penny found.

For a while I read a lot about manifesting. I followed all the steps. Nothing. But once I started coming out from under the rubble of my own subconscious, things really started to flow. I find now that I don't have to ask, pray, or hope for a lot of things. I wonder or mention and suddenly there it is, just what I need. Over and over again. I was recently walking back from the beach with a friend and questioned if we needed a third chair. There, within twenty feet, was a chair someone had left by the recycling. I'm not sure we can ask for flow. Live truly does flow around those who are blocked and easily through those who remove the blocks. I am forever grateful and constantly amazed.

Chapter Six

Breaking Down The Barriers.

Finding a fearlessly relentless commitment toward your own freedom.

In the previous chapters we've worked toward gaining a better understanding of why things have happened the way they have, and we've gotten a glimpse of what the future could hold. With that knowledge we should be able to move forward in significant ways, but will we?

Just as a huge pile of materials surrounded by an entire construction crew doesn't make a house, neither will the first five chapters make for a guaranteed transformation. Nor will moving through the rest of this book without picking up your tool bag, gathering your crew, and putting hammer to nail. Almost no single human being can embark on a journey of self-healing, self-love, and self-acceptance totally by themselves. But we can begin there, as long as we are willing to open our minds to the possibility of different perspectives.

So many of us have been surviving in waves. Many of us have a small collective of one or two people we can trust at times of vulnerability. Many of us have been so focused on financial security we haven't stopped long enough to even know what it may be like to have a circle of people we can trust on a deeply personal level.

And very often, if we've tied our very identities up with our financial worth or levels of production, fear can immobilize us completely. Especially when the ego strongly believes it is successful.

That's the really hideous thing about the false beliefs that have plagued us for so long and have often held us hostage; that we may be too panic-stricken to even consider another way forward. Fear can leave us holding that bag, consciously choosing to remain outside in the cold.

This is a form of fear-based denial. And once you realize that's all it is, why would you let it stop you any longer? When you shut down to even thinking about why you're so fearful or in denial and avoidance you shut down every possible opportunity to make the change you want. Denial is generally a fear-based embrace of victim mentality which creates opportunity for codependent behavior as you'll align yourself with people who enable you to retain your status as a victim. But if we stop and examine unwanted behaviors, we can see them for what they really are, vises of avoidant coping.

From this day on, at least one thing will be absolutely different for you. You now have a new awareness. If you are not making the changes you want you will need to consider why you are not willing to take the personal responsibility for yourself needed for change.

Once you have taken the steps this far, you now have the conscious ability to choose to take yourself forward. By now you can see that fear is simply an unprocessed set of emotions and lack of knowledge, not an actual threat to your security. And by continuing to part two you will gain many of the skills needed. There may be a few or even many things deeply hidden in your subconscious that you may need the help of a hypnotherapist accessing in order to release them, and that's okay. You may need to create a circle of trust, and that's okay.

But knowing all this now, why would you not take this journey? Who doesn't want more freedom? Who doesn't want more happiness? Why would you not want more success? What on earth is a good reason to continue to make unhealthy choices for yourself? What could possibly make you want to keep smoking those disgusting cigarettes that turn your teeth brown, your lungs black and your breath foul? Nothing about any of this makes you cool. Why would you continue to disconnect from your body and use food for comfort when it just makes you that much more uncomfortable in your own skin? Why would you continue to spend money on things you don't really care about when you dislike your job?

In the past, all of those have been fear-driven activities to assist in coping, that you did not purposefully choose for yourself. You continue to perpetuate them because your subconscious drives your thoughts, perceptions, and beliefs to be misaligned with your greater good. But now you can learn to access them as never before. Now you know where they live, why they lurk and the purpose they used to serve. Now you can see these sneaky little rat- bastards for the bullshit safety tools of a subconscious that's been left in the dark. You can now consciously bring it into the light.

The scale of your willingness to move onto a solid internal foundation and remove the need for excuses or external remedies can be very broad. We all fall somewhere on a chart that begins at "I'm not willing to do anything" and ends at "I'm willing to be fearless in my pursuit of the truth", and it's totally up to you. Ask yourself this; why are you so willing to break your ass for an employer and leave nearly no time for your own joy and happiness?

According to John Ruskan:

"When I accept myself and my feelings as they are I become whole. I am no longer split fighting - or condemning part of myself. The power of self-acceptance and self-love builds within me. I acquire the ability to heal myself and the conditions of my life. I awaken the power for transformation."

(Ruskan, 2006)

CONSCIOUSNESS IS UNDER THE RUBBLE

Who was it that told you money and achievement were the only way you would be of value? Stop and find out who it was, right now. You don't have to become anti- money or anti-anything. Anti is what brought us here. You just have to let go of the beliefs that are faulty which block and misdirect you. Money is fine, but it is not the only determining factor to live safe and happy lives. In fact, it has far less to do with either of those than you may imagine. Somewhere, hidden within each one of us are those bullshit beliefs, assumptions, and perspectives that trip us up and bind us to the old way of doing things. The underlying notions we accept as part of ourselves that have not once been worthy of our full-bodied embrace of their crap.

Open your mind to the way you see yourself. Challenge the way you value your time. Many of us feel guilty just taking time to rest on the couch and do nothing. We push ourselves to be our best outwardly but don't allow any real recovery time inwardly. Now is the time to start allowing yourself a little downtime. Re- group periodically to check in with yourself throughout the day. Allow yourself to review the workday prior to heading home so you can prepare yourself for family time. And consider building a support group. Not just a circle of trusted friends. A support group where you can completely be yourself and still be truly safe. We ALL need a support group; even emotionally intelligent and successful people can have support groups.

We move into the introspective work to increase emotional self-awareness and understand trauma resolution in Part Two. To prepare for this please make sure you have a quite comfortable space from which to work. Also, there will be a fair amount of writing involved. We have left space in the question section as well as several pages in the back for writing. Otherwise, your choice of a journal, laptop or note pad will be needed.

Please remember how important both your safe space is as well as doing the work. Take as many breaks as needed but don't set the work aside for long if you feel comfortable to continue without the help of a professional. It's so easy to hide from ourselves in avoidance and distraction. But the ability to be fully present far more often than not will be worth your time to finish the materials and continue your personal journey back to your soul.

Author's notes: A shiny new Penny

For so long, six decades, my thoughts were infused with the shame of being overweight. My parents thoroughly shamed me, causing me to shut down emotionally at age seven or eight. I could be writing about weight issues or could have turned my focus elsewhere entirely.

When I learned how important emotional self-awareness really is and how much it affects all aspects of life, I felt a drive and passion like never before. Uncovering what drives our actions and removing the pain that drives ugliness can change so many things.

I can't count the number of times I've let other people's bullshit affect how I feel. About myself, my abilities, who I am and how I am in the world. It can be so hard to stay in your own lane after all the indoctrination and years of living with those beliefs.

What we have to keep fresh in our minds is our own responsibility to ourselves has to be the most important priority. When we become responsible for how we feel, we can more easily notice when someone is projecting their stuff on to us. We can more easily remember that it comes from their own place of feeling less than, feeling insecure and wanting to diminish others to for their own benefit.

When we feel responsible for ourselves, fully accountable to ourselves first, we can manage our feelings to lessen anxiety and control our behavior far more easily. Without allowing our emotional selves be assaulted or abused we can insulate and protect ourselves before the subconscious tries to drive us to drink (or another obsession!)

CONSCIOUSNESS IS UNDER THE RUBBLE

And the more we step back from what anyone else is trying to project, the more they will have to begin to question themselves or at the very least stop trying to bully us in their process.

Part Two

Building And Maintaining Emotional Self- Awareness In Professional And Personal Environments: Tools, Strategies, And Exercises.

Chapter Seven

Understanding ARMS.

As highlighted in Part One of this book, the three things that keep us from living a mindful conscious lifestyle are unreleased programming, unresolved trauma, and the inability to manage ourselves emotionally. Part Two of this book looks further into these three things, approaching it from two different lenses: self and supporter. The first lens of self looks from within to develop strategies and exercises to become more emotionally self-aware. The second lens of supporters examines how our outwardly focusing roles encourage others in becoming more emotionally aware. This section will provide different resources to consider in the introduction to basic emotional self-awareness.

The foundation of this support and provided resources is based on an acronym we refer to as ARMS. ARMS also has a figurative meaning in how our arms can connect to provide a supportive space to allow for emotional awareness to occur. This provides a genuine and safe space for support in taking the journey in basic awareness. The acronym meaning of ARMS is:

Assess - Personal self-awareness is what allows us to see through old, outdated ideologies. It's the thing that allows us to step out of the daily drama and get a breath of fresh air to regroup and assess our own presence. This first focus is to truly assess your own presence of where you are today as it relates to your emotional awareness.

Reflection - Understanding dysfunctional patterns and their origins are the key to unlocking unwanted behavior. Without the ability to take responsibility for ourselves emotionally, we have given our own personal power away in a myriad of ways. The second focus is to reflect on your past in order to locate the root causes of things that block your emotional awareness and progress today.

Making this connection internally unlocks each of the times you've been unable to explain your behavior or your choices. It will finally make sense of the times you've given your best and found sustainable change still illusive. Uncovering the role of the subconscious, accessing all of the repressed emotional energy, and releasing each piece is what brings the freedom of acceptance. It's what clears the path to conscious living. As you move through these exercises and begin to lighten your emotional baggage you may notice massive shifts in perspectives. Knowing where to access the blocks and gaining the skills and tools to master them releases you from that lifelong state of frustration almost all of us have encountered.

Manage - In order to put ourselves back in charge of our choices, we must become more aware of the patterns of our behaviors and their origins. Personal growth of this type is a process. It won't happen overnight. It won't happen if you ignore any of the steps because the subconscious will continually pull you back into the safety of the comfort zone if you do. The third focus is to implement a plan to further develop your emotional awareness that is realistic with the understanding that it is not a change that will happen in a short amount of time and must continue to include ongoing reflection moments to make modifications as needed.

Support - Until you take time to find a safe way to unpack and unload what you've been carrying, you cannot be free. The degree to which we feel safe leads that charge. The safer you feel, the more comfortable you will be with vulnerability. The more fearful you are, the more defensive you will become. The fourth focus is to make sure to create and maintain a support system that includes safe spaces and support to continue to further your emotional awareness to live in a more grounded space.

Before you begin the exercises, think back to the introduction. What was the thing/s you called out as your nemesis? Remember to get clear on that as it will be needed throughout these exercises.

Chapter Eight

Assess

The first part of ARMS is to ASSESS where you are now. This beginning to the basic understanding of emotional awareness focuses on what you have experienced previously in life and how you have reacted to those experiences. Assessing your starting point focuses only on a basic understanding of emotional self-awareness in order to move forward to create a better space for you in life.

The Importance of Emotional Self-Awareness - Research suggests the importance of emotional awareness from a theoretical perspective (Smith, R., Killgore, W.D.S., & Lane R.D., 2018). So often, many of us have been trained to ignore our own emotions as children that we have not been taught how to properly manage them as adults. In childhood, when we feel pain or fear that has been ignored by our trusted adults, (we are told to be quiet or that we are okay) it sends a subliminal message telling us how we feel does not matter. Without explanation or the ability to process, this message creates a consistent flow of low-level anxiety. The subconscious then will often choose to place disconnect between our souls from our bodies in order to protect us and allow us to continue moving forward with life the best way possible. As we age and further advance into society, the need to conform to and for others begins to outweigh our ability to stay in touch with our soul or its purpose.

CONSCIOUSNESS IS UNDER THE RUBBLE

To begin, let's think about the following questions and how they affect your day-to-day emotional awareness. On a document or journal, please write as much as you can for each of the questions:

What has been your understanding of the role that emotions play in your day-to-day life?

What are some good examples of how you've been able to identify emotions in your life?

Can you list some areas where you feel stuck in your life? If yes, list them. Write as deeply as possible, connecting with each area and try to locate the belief keeping you stuck. What are some areas where you'd like to experience change or gain? List them here:

What are the specific emotions were provoked by the last things you listed?

Can you identify a time earlier in life when you felt those same emotions? Noticing the connections and how linking current feelings connects your actions back to past pain points.

As explained in Part One, upon examination, we find society as a whole has lacked the proper training of the management of emotions overall. Imagine walking into a job you believe you are ready for; you've had the initial training and are excited to get started. Now imagine that you find yourself being expected to uphold the duties of a much higher level of training or skill set than you possess. This is what has happened to so many of us when it comes to our ability to navigate emotions properly. We've not been trained to balance the internal and external parts of life correctly.

To support the information shared in this chapter, an online course has been provided to assist you further in gaining a better understanding of basic emotional awareness. Access to the free course is located at https:// unpackingemotionalbaggage.com/

The free course includes the following:

Module 1: Basic Emotional Awareness

Understanding emotional awareness. Your emotional selves go with you wherever you go, whether you like it or not. In childhood, many are encouraged to ignore their emotions.

Module 2: Increasing Personal Awareness

Increase awareness that relates to self. Give yourself permission to feel and equip yourself with the tools to navigate your emotions properly. This can be accomplished in three phases: identifying an emotion, understanding, and processing, and releasing the emotion.

Module 3: Taking Agency

Having the skills/tools to properly navigate and manage your own emotions. Personal growth demands you take agency. Taking agency is defined as "the capacity of individuals to act independently and make their own free choices."

Module 4: Our Social Awareness

The ability to take full responsibility for how you feel at any given time. How to access your own empathy. Allowing others to be responsible for their emotions. The ability to self- regulate with frequent emotional check-ins throughout the day.

This approach to learning about basic emotional awareness acknowledges there are other aspects to an individual that should be considered as a holistic understanding of individuals.

CONSCIOUSNESS IS UNDER THE RUBBLE

If you find you are experiencing significant levels of discomfort as you move through these materials, it is strongly recommended that you seek out additional support. Please refer to the following information to get additional resources to support you in this journey.

National Institute of Mental Health
https:// www.nimh.nih.gov/health/find-help
National Alliance on Mental Health - www.nami.org Suicide Prevention
www.suicidepreventionlifeline.org (800) 273-TALK (8255)

Chapter Nine

Reflection.

The second part of ARMS is REFLECTION. Research has identified the importance of understanding the levels of emotional awareness (Lane, R. D., & Schwartz, G. E. (1987). Self-reflection is an extremely valuable tool as we travel toward emotional awareness. As we navigate this journey, our perspectives will shift as we gain more awareness and increase our levels of consciousness.

It's important to reflect on the things we've considered the most important in life thus far as our starting point to note our current priorities in life. Then we can begin to reflect on what levels of success we've achieved on each of the things we currently value.

Before we begin, let's take a look at any false beliefs you may still carry regarding the importance of emotional self-awareness. Think about each of the next set of questions and place a check mark next to the beliefs that apply. This will help you determine any false belief systems you've been relying upon.

- Feelings don't matter, they have no value.
- Emotions are to be ignored or buried.
- Feelings are not to be trusted.
- Emotions are to be feared.
- Being emotional makes you vulnerable.

- Showing emotions make you look weak.

Continue to write any additional fears you may have self- identified.

The importance of self-analysis for balance in life.

Because the road to adulting often doesn't allow sufficient time for contemplation or self-reflection, we often begin forging our way forward and never look back. It's extremely likely that more balance is needed between placing importance on financial security and personal empowerment that the levels of emotional self- awareness we enter adulthood provides. To be balanced we must be able to give equal priority internally as we do externally, especially in the ways we seek remedy.

The lack of self-reflection can take us down roads we have not chosen, causing life to be lived by default for lengthy periods of time. We often find ourselves entering adulthood bearing great responsibilities, many times for things we've not been trained to handle at all.

With so much focus of the past having been on external accomplishments and financial security to bring about balance we must turn inward to find a true sense of deeper internal peace as well as personal power. By focusing on current priorities and values the following exercises will bring clarity around the current status of balance in your life today.

Think of things you have accomplished thus far in life. This can include past accomplishments, goals you have reached, milestones, etc. List them:

CONSCIOUSNESS IS UNDER THE RUBBLE

Take a few minutes to reflect on each of the accomplishments you've listed, one at a time. Write how each one affected you on an emotional level as you reached your goals. Ask yourself if the accomplishment brought you the expected joy or happiness. If so, how sustainable have those feelings been. Now reflect on the desires you have ahead of you in life and list the things you would still like to accomplish below.

Now, reflecting back on the levels of sustainability derived from your past achievements, write how much sustainable happiness and joy you expect from your list of desires. Close your eyes and visualize how these accomplishments will affect your day-to-day life. How will these changes bring more lasting happiness, peace, or freedom?

We are often so focused on forward motion that the expectations of our accomplishments don't result in the lasting joy or happiness we'd hoped for, which leaves us continually seeking. Whether it is a bigger house, a new car, a better vacation, or a next pay increase, we continue to seek. We get stuck in the loop of thought that tells us once we get the next and the next after that we will be happy. This is a result of seeking all gratification externally which leaves us still wanting more internally. This is why self-reflection is so important in keeping both internal and external focus in balance. Without the internal connection we will continue to seek. Without understanding the importance of looking inward the focus will be external. The loop of distraction will continue.

For the next exercise, turn your focus internally. Think of personal things you'd like to have more of in your life. Things on this list may include more joy, happiness, inner peace, deeper connections, better relationships, more freedom, or a job you love.

List the top things you personally desire here:

Now that you have written them down, it is important to understand that there can be many variables that impact how we exist. For this book, we will only focus on the emotional blocks with the understanding there are other variables that contribute to our life experiences.

Imagining the difference between the two lists, the second and more personal one may seem further out of reach because the things blocking that path can be more deeply hidden. Stop and connect at a deeper level to those personal desires. Picture them in place in your life moving forward. Imagine the impact on your day-to-day life, in your relationships, in your values. Reflect more on this here:

Turn your focus toward the specific reasons that would block you from your internal personal desires. Examine each and determine if they are emotional blocks or physical blocks. For example, imagine you would like to start your own businesses once your values have shifted. There are emotional blocks and physical blocks you would have to overcome. Some of the physical blocks would be the money to start the business, getting the proper approvals for the business, and so on. Some of the emotional blocks would be fear of failure, fear of financial loss, and so forth.

Emotional blocks will naturally be harder to determine and examine as we've been primarily focused on the exterior in the past. Consider the following:

CONSCIOUSNESS IS UNDER THE RUBBLE

<u>Personal blocks</u> of insecurity are rooted in the hurt, fear, and confusion of the past.

<u>Conditioned personal beliefs</u> are created by messaging we received in our youth that resulted in false beliefs about ourselves personally, our ability and our worth or value as humans.

<u>Conditioned social beliefs</u> are things such as the indoctrination of hatred, religious beliefs, supremacy, education, politics, and so on.

Using the above information, please review your list of future desires from the previous activity and list both the emotional and physical blocks you can identify at this time:

Let's dig deeper into our indoctrinated belief systems now, as they can easily minimize our emotional awareness by minimizing our own worth and value.

A few examples of personal false beliefs and negative internal narratives are: I am not worthy.

- I am too emotional.
- I am unattractive.
- I am too sensitive.
- Nobody likes me.
- I am weak.
- I am not intelligent.

Look back at the list of blocks, take a moment to close your eyes and reflect back to your childhood in reference to false belief.

Look for things that connect the dots between your childhood experiences and the blocks you listed. An example would be your parents saying no to most things you asked for as a child and a fear of spending money on yourself as an adult. Using the next questions as prompts, write about how each belief has affected your life in a less than positive way. How much truth does each hold?

What emotion, pain or fear comes up around each of those false beliefs? How do each of those statements minimize you personally?

Write in-depth why you still believe any of the statements and why you may be giving them so much power.

Think about how each one of them makes you feel in vivid detail. Think about why you feel that way. Identify and describe those feelings.

Now think about the very first time you felt those feelings in the past. List those below:

Look for the connections between the current block and what part of the past it connected you back to via the emotions you felt. Write down as much as you can about that connection. Pay specific attention to any light bulb moments or revelations you have. For some, this may be your introduction to journaling. For others, a new way to connect the dots between the past indoctrination and present real-time blocks. Every block links to a piece of repressed pain or false belief which is deeply rooted somewhere in the past. Each will result in some type of limitation you will see in your day-to-day life. They will appear as a fear, insecurity, or belief that what you want is not for you. The emotions that are attached to the limitations you encounter will reflect back to past unreleased energy. Those emotions, when examined and understood, will guide you back to a place where the unreleased energy can be processed and released. Once it's no longer hiding, it can no longer block you.

These tools may be all you need to open up your awareness and start the healing process, however the help of a professional may be needed. There are times when we simply cannot access the specific pain that needs healing and that's ok.

Give yourself a high-five and take a well-earned break before continuing on with the rest of Part Two.

Chapter Ten

Manage.

The third part of ARMS is to MANAGE. Managing our emotional awareness is important in maintaining our progress and continuing down the road toward emotional intelligence and a conscious lifestyle. One of the best approaches is to have frequent check-ins with yourself throughout your day.

As you think about the questions below, it is important that you understand the differences between reacting emotionally and responding calmly.

Reacting emotionally is when an individual feels hurt, which can cause a trigger. A trigger happens anytime an old, unresolved pain point has been activated causing the subconscious to implement an impulsive or compulsive reaction or behavior; often overreacting, which can be viewed as a state of fight or flight. Responding calmly is when an individual stays in control, acknowledges and diffuses the situation in a calm manner.

Reflection Questions

Reflect on a time you've been frustrated with choices you have made or times when you have wanted to make changes and have failed. List those experiences here.

CONSCIOUSNESS IS UNDER THE RUBBLE

Can you think of a time when you managed an instance poorly? How might you manage that differently now?

Think of a time you were confused or concerned about how to properly manage a situation. What were the circumstances? How comfortable were you about asking for help at that time? How well do you understand your own personal triggers? What measures do you take to manage or distract from them?

The importance of triggers - A trigger is like an emotional land mind that makes us explode when touched upon. The purpose of triggers is twofold. Once we encounter a familiar pain point, the subconscious moves into safety mode seeking ways to soothe us. But more importantly, once investigated, that trigger will lead us back to the original pain point when we use a little introspection. Just as you did in one of the earlier journaling exercises, you can use the emotions surrounding the real-time trigger to trace them back to the original pain point by remembering the first time you felt that same emotion. This is how you locate the root of the trigger.

In recalling a story of an inmate who described a triggering event in his book Daniel Goleman says: "Such emotional explosions are neural hijackings. At those moments, evidence suggests, a center in the limbic brain proclaims an emergency, recruiting the rest of the brain to its urgent agenda. The hijacking occurs in an instant, triggering this reaction at crucial moments before the neocortex, the thinking brain, has a chance to glimpse fully what is happening, let alone decide if it is a good idea."

(Goleman, 2005)

The importance of self-regulation - Because many of us have not been trained to understand emotions: we don't know how to identify, process, release, and regulate them properly and we turn to distraction and denial in avoidance. Avoidant coping methods are often dysfunctional, self-destructive behaviors that further remove us from our personal power and agency.

There are many strategies that can be implemented to reduce the risk of avoidance coping. Carefully review the next list. Think about what you already practice and what you can start implementing in your daily life. Also, consider what you know will not work for you based on your own personal preferences and past experiences when trying to implement new practices.

- Implement routine daily assessments of your emotions.
- Establish healthy self-care methods as a top priority.
- Ensure you have adequate guilt-free rest.
- Respect your time as well as the time of others.
- Limiting the unnecessary daily drama of life.
- Develop and maintain self-efficacy.
- Understand, establish, and maintain strong boundaries.
- Accept that change takes time and release an all or- nothing mentality.

Recognize the role of the subconscious. Implement replacements for its role of security guard, such as proper coping skills. Consider how you will navigate relationships when your level of emotional self-awareness rises and others may not.

Limit outside media stressors.

The importance of the re-frame.

Many experiences that are hard to let go of and keep us looping in the same thoughts need to be healed. One of the hardest things to hear is "just let it go" when a negative experience persists, and you can't find ways to navigate the problem. These are often very personal and painful instances concerning another person who is unavailable or unwilling to participate.

Re-framing works a lot like forgiveness. Forgiving someone for their actions and re-framing your perspective brings peace to the forgiver without having to involve the other person. This is how you take back your power from the other person. Remember, the only person you can change is yourself. There is no healthy benefit in holding onto anger and resentment. We don' t need to make sense of their journey, only how they have impacted our lives. To re-frame, you will need a safe, quiet space where you will not be interrupted. Please remember that you will need to have processed and resolved any serious anger you feel toward this person beforehand, there is no place in re-framing for vengeance. The purpose here is to create inner peace around the situation.

Put yourself in the most comfortable position possible, relax, and begin to think about the other person and the feelings that have lingered. Re-framing is a two- part process. First, envision what you have been wanting to say and see yourself saying it face-to-face with the other person. Take as long as you want, allowing for the emotions to flow and release as much as you safely can. Say everything until you feel complete and relieved. Second, envision the person saying everything you have been hoping to hear from them. Part of this type of healing is putting ourselves in a position to accept that the other person cannot meet us in a healing place. Using acceptance in conjunction with the tools to re-frame, we can move back into our personal power and find a peaceful reprieve. Because giving our power to a situation we cannot change depletes our energy with no benefit to ourselves in any way.

Making space for yourself to clear the air and get closure is the best self-care you can practice when you are unable to do the repair or healing work you desire with the other person who is involved. Remember, you are the person you live with, not the person who lingers in your thoughts. Reframing to bring yourself peace quiets the mind and heals the heart. If this practice doesn't release you, look deeper into identifying the residual feelings that need further work to process and release.

The importance of self-care.

As we have often been discouraged from fully engaging with our internal selves, it's not uncommon for selfcare to be mistaken for selfishness, which is a false belief. Self-serving means serving one's own interests often in disregard to the truth or the interests of others. Self- care means to care for oneself by acknowledging yourself as a primary concern in your own life.

Self-care is encouraged as part of understanding emotional awareness. The lack of self-serving can hinder the understanding and development of emotional awareness.

Self-care is one of the most important aspects of maintaining balance in our day-to-day lives. It doesn't need to be rooted in high-maintenance, high-cost routines. Often, regimented services once considered pampering adds anxiety rather than alleviating it.

A few sample self-care activities to consider, also pay attention to resistance you may feel towards any:

- Pay attention to emotions as they arise.
- Make healthy choices when planning meals.
- Get regular exercise (or consider why you may be avoiding it).
- Prioritize rest and relaxation.
- Create more time with those we connect deeply with.
- Recognize and eliminate toxic situations.
- Maintain healthy boundaries.

List the areas you'd like to experience elevated levels of self-care. Beside each, list any reasons that may block you from attaining those levels. Use your journal to further examine those blocks and reflect on what supports are needed to reach these levels:

Chapter Eleven

Support.

The fourth part of ARMS is to SUPPORT. The fourth focus is to intentionally create and maintain a support system that includes safe spaces, which will guide and ground you as you continue your personal growth journey.

Some initial aspects to consider in creating a successful system are here:

- Creating safe spaces internally at any time or place.
- Creating a circle of positive energy.
- Understanding how to monitor environmental changes.
- Understanding how to maintain safe spaces.

Reflection questions:

How willing are you to accept support in your life?

How confident are you that others can create a space that is safe for you?

CONSCIOUSNESS IS UNDER THE RUBBLE

How do you seek out support to discuss emotional awareness challenges?

Take time now to answer the reflection questions above in your favorite means of journaling. Next list some ways that you envision creating a safe space of your own and those who may be invited into your circle of trust and support.

Now, think about circumstances that you may find yourself in when you could become too overwhelmed to create a safe space for yourself. Write on that here: Think about the people in your life who may distract you or even discourage you from keeping healthy boundaries. List the top possible disruptors below:

Going back to your journaling process, or simply next to each item, write down your remedies. Close your eyes and really envision yourself in the tensest of situations and see yourself taking those deep breaths, feel your energy shift, and step back into your personal power. Write how you accomplished those changes.

Taking time to prepare for potentially intense situations can be helpful in preventing the loss of power and maintaining strong and safe boundaries. This is one of the very best methods of uplifting yourself and your energy. So, go for it! Preview that meeting with your boss in the car before you arrive. Have the talk you've been needing to have with your mother or your spouse. Review the best way to navigate a tricky situation with your children. The more negative energy you remove prior to the event the better the outcome.

Continue to build your support. The format of a successful support system can be established in various modalities that include online, in-person, or a hybrid of both. In addition, the support system should allow for interactive one-on-one and group opportunities.

Chapter Twelve

ARMS for others.

The future leaders will be those who have come out of denial, who have dug deeply, fearlessly, and relentlessly into releasing any baggage that was holding them back. They will have found their way back to empathy and compassion in their relentless pursuit of their truth. The future currency in the job market will be emotional self-awareness and the world will heal as social-emotional competency becomes mainstream.

As you heal and grow, so does your ability to guide others along their own journeys. In this section of Part Two, we will discuss how to provide support to others in our roles of leaders, educators, caregivers, and other hierarchical roles.

It is important you understand what your expected role is in this journey to support others. This will include your understanding of self-efficacy and which role you will assume specifically related to basic emotional awareness. Self-efficacy is one's own ability to lead themselves toward a specific goal or outcome. This includes multiple factors when taking a holistic approach. It could include resiliency, physical determination, society status, emotional awareness, personality characteristics, etc. For the purpose of this book, self-efficacy will focus on an individual's level of self-directedness.

CONSCIOUSNESS IS UNDER THE RUBBLE

Understanding an individual's level of self-directedness will assist you in understanding how to support them to achieve basic emotional awareness. In general, self- directedness is a spectrum in which an individual needs close directed support to minimum directed support to achieve an individual goal. One of the preferred models to use is Grow's Self-Directed Model.

Grow's Staged Self-Directed Learning (SSDL) model outlines how teachers can help students become more self-directed in their learning (Grow, 1991). Grow identifies four stages of the self-directed learner to assist facilitators in successfully working with learners to become self-directed learners:

Stage 1: Dependent learner - Learners of low self-direction who need an authority figure (a teacher) to tell them what to do.

Stage 2: Interested learner - Learners of moderate self- direction who are motivated and confident but largely ignorant of the subject matter to be learned. The teacher motivates and guides the learner.

Stage 3: Involved learner - Learners of intermediate self- direction who have both the skill and the basic knowledge and who view themselves as being both ready and able to explore a specific area with a good guide. The teacher facilitates as an equal in the learning environment.

Stage 4: Self-directed learner - Learners of high self- direction who are both willing and able to plan, execute, and evaluate their own learning with or without the help of an expert. The teacher cultivates the student's ability to learn.

(Grow, 1991)

Before proceeding with ARMs, it is important to understand at which stage of self-directed learning the individual self-assesses so that the appropriate support is provided to gain a level of basic emotional awareness. It is recommended that the individual complete the survey at the link below and share the information with you so that you can determine your role in supporting the individual on this journey.

A Self-Directed Self-Assessment can be at www.unpackingemotionalbaggage.com.

Assess key points.

Similar to your own experience in gaining a basic emotional awareness, others need to assess where they are as they begin. Similar to what you completed in the first section of Part Two, the same free online course needs to be completed by the individual you are supporting. Your role will shift as support for others. It is your responsibility to actively listen while understanding your own biases and life experiences so as to not project them onto the individuals you are supporting. It is also crucial that you understand the importance of verbally acknowledging and validating the emotions being shared with you, just as we must learn to pay attention to our emotions on a regular basis until it becomes natural.

One effective way to not project your own experiences is to reflect back on the activity you completed in the MANAGE sections of ARMS. Key factors that directly influence our levels of emotional self-awareness are:

- Past experiences (primarily those from childhood).
- The ability to understand and navigate emotions.
- Self-assessment of strategies for anxiety, triggers, etc.
- Environmental factors.

As you keep in perspective your biases, you should actively listen to the individual you are supporting to facilitate an open and accepting conversation and not direct it in any manner. It is also important that you understand what role you are assuming from the self- directed learning model previously discussed in this section, such as:

- Authority Figure
- Motivator
- Facilitator as an Equal
- Cultivator

Please note that your role can and will change as both you and the individual assumes different levels of emotional self-awareness.

The free course is located at
https:// unpackingemotionalbaggage.com/

Reflection key points.

As stated in Part One, self-reflection is important in starting the road toward emotional awareness. You should support the individual using the same exercises you've completed. As you work with the individual you are supporting, review the individual reflections in the free course and consider the additional questions below:

- How open is the person to doing the work?
- What level of the spectrum are they on from acceptance to denial?
- What is their level of emotional self-awareness?
- How much self-exploration and clearing of trauma and insecurities have they completed? How much does the person understand about emotions?
- Do they know the basics of how to identify, process, and release feelings on their own?
- Are they aware enough to do self-check-ins during the day and as things arise on an emotional level?
- How big is the person's false self?
- Are they projecting their beliefs as truths?
- Do they deny that they have any work to do on themselves at all?

CONSCIOUSNESS IS UNDER THE RUBBLE

While we hear more about mental health, there is a significant difference between psychological damage and emotional distress. Unless properly trained we can only assist in supporting others when it comes to emotional matters, for matters outside of our abilities assist them in seeking out professional support to best assist them.

One approach to supporting others is to encourage them to purchase a journal and create a routine to write in it every day. The other option is to use an app or your laptop. Make sure it is secure and that no one else can access it. The journal should focus on reflection; however, the person feels best to include the information. It is important to know that this is a safe space to share all your thoughts that can include your frustrations. This could include pictures, drawings, quotes, and other methods of an individual's preferred method of self- reflection. To get the individual to start journaling, provide them with the following prompts:

- What was a highlight of the day?
- What was a challenging part of the day?
- What events impacted you the most emotionally?
- If you encountered an uncomfortable situation, how did you react to it?
- What do you want to focus on for tomorrow to maintain your emotional awareness?

Manage key points.

As a supporter, your role is to assist others in understanding the different choices of management tools and perspectives. It is not your role to select what is best for the individual. However, depending on your self- directed role, you might have to be more involved in walking through the different options and directing the person to reflect on each option and share their level of comfort or discomfort along with the reason for the level of comfort. The following management tools/ perspectives discussed earlier in this section that are related to emotional awareness are:

- Developing and maintaining self-efficacy.
- Understanding strong boundaries.
- Stop ignoring your emotional self (daily assessment).
- Establishing self-care as a priority.
- Ensuring you have adequate rest.
- Understanding how to get the subconscious tools to stand down (soothing yourself outside of your comfort zone).
- Releasing all or nothing mentality. Determining how to manage when you start outgrowing people.
- Creating a daily check on your level of emotional challenges.
- Practicing not getting caught up in the drama.

Support key points.

It is important for the individual to understand you are not the only person that can support them in understanding and maintaining emotional awareness. A major aspect to remember is to hold a safe space without being distracted.

In order to hold a space that is beneficial and fully supportive of another, we need to provide a safe space that is free of judgment, criticism, and any type of projection of our beliefs, values, or perceptions. We also need to ensure we are participating as an active listener, free of our own internal distractions, such as:

- Any need to fix the problem or have the answer.
- Forward thinking pertaining to our story and not theirs.
- Interrupting during conversations.
- Reactions to our own personal triggers.

Part Three provides more insight on how to continue to support ourselves and each other as we continue on our personal journeys.

Part Three

Hope For The Future, From Clueless To Conscious.

Sustainable change brings sustainable inner peace, happiness, joy, and freedom.

Chapter Thirteen

Evolution Is A Lifelong Process.

"The more I learn, the more I realize how much I don't know." —
Albert Einstein

Once a journey of personal growth begins in earnest, it will become a continuum of new revelations. Identifying and unpacking emotional baggage is a process that will eventually lead you to a place of ever-expanding consciousness and a sense of deeper peace.

The journey will be filled with trials, tests, and a lot of the unexpected! As a person's emotional foundation becomes sturdier and our social narratives more fluid, it is important to pay close attention to our balance, internally and externally as we progress. Remember to keep in mind that the subconscious has had a long history of being in charge. It's not going to walk away quietly! It will still seek to protect us. It will revert back to seeing accumulation and productivity as our means of our security. And will continue to keep pushing us right past many of life's meaningful moments.

To move out of this trap, we continually have to prove to the subconscious that we are ready to manage our emotions. We have to do the work of reclaiming power consciously, one trigger and one block at a time. This calls for another level of awareness and the potential need to re-center in each situation.

It's important to recognize that at times of overwhelm, the subconscious is still looking to keep us safe. It's not just seeking out a way to soothe us of pain, it's also seeking a way to avoid confusion because confusion was also a part of our childhood experience. Being overwhelmed is confusing and can easily pull us right back into old patterns. Even after gaining great levels of emotional self-awareness and personal power from clearing the subconscious of fear, pain, and beliefs a person can become overwhelmed. Which makes self- assessment that much more important to avoid triggers and setbacks. In his book, Dr. van der Kolb explains "In later years I encountered a similar phenomenon in the victims of child abuse: Most of them suffered from agonizing shame about the actions they took to survive and maintain a connection with the person who abused them. That was particularly true if the abuser was someone close to the child, someone the child depended on, as is so often the case. The result can be confusion about whether one was a victim or a willing participant, which leads to bewilderment about the difference between love and terror, pain, and pleasure."

(Dr. van der Kolb, 2015)

Emotional self-awareness is our best friend and most trusted ally all through our life. Any of the tools highlighted in part two can be referred to as needed at any time. In order to not fall back into old well-patterned behaviors, it is extremely important to keep these factors in mind at all times:

- Self-assessment is a superpower.
- Maintaining your ability to identify, process, and release emotions as they appear.
- The importance of providing a safe space for yourself. Making physical and emotional rest a priority for your success.
- Assuming full responsibility for your actions and emotions.

- Creating and upholding firm boundaries.
- Recognizing that overwhelm and uncertainty can also be triggers.

The more comfortable we are with our understanding and acceptance of ourselves the more comfortable we naturally become with others. When we take responsibility for our emotions we empower ourselves and no longer give anyone the power to affect us on an emotional level because we have put the tools in place necessary to navigate these situations.

From that solid foundation, we can make informed decisions about who we can trust and rely upon. At the same time, we must allow that our relationships may change as we grow, and our levels of personal growth are no longer equal to those around us.

Friends, family, and co-workers will be biased in how they have come to understand and accept you. When you step far outside the boundaries of other people's comfort zones they may be triggered. As we grow and our priorities and perspectives change, so will our relationships.

If you're not solely focused in a deep pursuit of money, if you fearlessly choose to embrace your emotions, if your path is about making yourself and the world better, those around you may be caught off guard. They may choose to remain trapped in outdated perceptions. And that's okay.

Personal growth and the deeper levels of understanding we have for our true selves and the work of our souls help us emerge from long-standing insecurities and false sets of beliefs. Once we know ourselves and what we want for ourselves we can free ourselves from the toxicity of manipulative and dysfunctional relationships. Without the pain points calling out for healing, we have now provided our souls with an open place to soar freely. From here it becomes natural to make conscious, mindful choices which are driven by self-love, instead of seeking the external validation of self-serving importance.

CONSCIOUSNESS IS UNDER THE RUBBLE

The internal reflective work of understanding our own baggage and unpacking it allows our soul to peek back out from under the watchful eye of the subconscious. This journey is not only about being authentically in who you are but also recognizing that your soul was fully on display when you were first born. The authenticity we seek as humans is that personal connection to our very soul. It's not been lost; it's only been under the rubble.

When those around us don't choose a path of introspection and don't process and release the insecurities of past pain and confusion they are likely to remain self-serving and unaware. And remember that self-serving choices are driven by those insecurities along with a lack of emotional self-awareness.

Author's notes: Picking up the Pennies.

Uncovering the reasons behind our behaviors may not always be top of mind. Over time we become so used to being who we learned to believe ourselves to be. Sometimes no matter how much work we do, we can forget to question our actions. I found out that when we don't question our limitations we can be missing out on some many wonderful things.

Even after I moved into new ways of life, sometimes the old bullshit still popped up, even after a decade of work. I had disliked sewing as a kid because it was almost all I was allowed for myself, and it meant I had to make my own clothing. That combined with the time I cut all the hair off of my first doll and then wasn't trusted to have anything new again, created an unrecognized limitation.

I'd been watching a reel of someone dissembling clothing and combining pieces. They turned out like works of art. It was fantastic. But when I sat down with two shirts and a pair of scissors I was frozen. It took me a while to piece together the two reasons but once I broke through I've been creating some pretty darn cute stuff myself.

CONSCIOUSNESS IS UNDER THE RUBBLE

This happened again shortly afterwards with a bike. If you read my first book you will already be familiar with how limited physical activity was for me as a kid. My first and only bike was something my dad pieced together out of scraps from the dump. It was too small for me by the time it was finished which led to some pretty embarrassing situations.

As I began looking for a beach cruiser I stared looking at used bikes for the lowest price. It wasn't until I read about one that required service that I paid attention to what I was doing. My first though was that I didn't want to get a bike serviced. It stopped me in my tracks. Why? Wasn't I worth a serviceable bike? I refined my search and limited it to only those that were the exact color I wanted and like new. I found the exact perfect bike and I love. It. But I sure had to think about those blocks to get where I really wanted to be for myself!

Chapter Fourteen

Social Consciousness.

Consciousness and emotional competency are the glue for all humanity.

Most emotional blockages begin early in life. Turning away from ourselves at a young age leaves us disconnected internally and unable to make strong connections with others, which can naturally lead to social anxiety. Being taught that emotions are to be ignored at an early age causes us to block our emotional selves as well as our ability to empathize.

Social-emotional competency is the ability to interact with others well. It contains elements of conflict resolution, acceptance, and a solid personal foundation. It helps us avoid anxiety in social situations and helps us be able to interact:

- With mutual respect.
- While maintaining and respecting boundaries. While actively listening with focused interest.
- Without projecting an internal agenda or the use of manipulative tactics.
- By recognizing personal triggers and responding calmly. By showing compassion, empathy, and kindness.

- Showing acceptance without judgment, even if we disagree.
- Replacing expectations of how someone should be with acceptance of how they are.

Now that we are on the path toward having a solid personal foundation we can begin to look outward and talk about how we can become ambassadors of emotional self-awareness and conscious lifestyles. As we have seen, we cannot be good leaders without a healthy and strong foundation from which to lead. Otherwise, our agenda reverts back to self-serving and self-aggrandizing with a focus on outdated and polarizing themes. Tools to repair and restore relationships - At times of disagreement, we may need to step back and work through our own processing of the circumstances before further engaging with others. Once all of the parties are ready, the tools to repair a relationship are very similar to some of the things that define social-emotional competency:

- Acknowledge that your emotions are your responsibility. Identify, process, and release your feelings beforehand.
- Accept the other person unconditionally for who they are.
- Arrange your time for an open-minded, open-hearted conversation; do not be defensive.
- Show up to actively listen without trying to fix or control things.
- Acknowledge and validate the other person's feelings. Uphold your boundaries.

The importance of emotional self-awareness in parenting - The importance of childhood experiences has been documented in terms of trauma for at least the past fifty years. However, the reluctance toward deeper self- reflection has been steadfast. One of the most overlooked forms of trauma is neglecting to verbally acknowledge and validate a child's worry before focusing on teaching them to become strong and resilient.

CONSCIOUSNESS IS UNDER THE RUBBLE

To begin raising generations who need less healing and have solid foundations as they become adults, understanding self-reflection is vital. Healthy competent parenting demands kindness, empathy, and compassion toward the children. It demands the parents find solid ground from which to guide them. Children in their most vulnerable states, count on adults to provide complete and total safety. They are desperate for deep unconditional love and acceptance.

Children's heart's desire parents who believe in them and homes where mistakes are treated as teachable moments. A child's life is not the place for the unfulfilled dreams and passions of the adult parents to be lived out or shortfalls to be overcome. Any expectations of or for the child need to be for their personal best interest.

Open and honest two-way conversations (talk with not to) need to be had so that the child is never left confused, hurt, or scared. Most of all, children need to be supported emotionally and taught how to understand their emotions and manage them confidently.

Increased individual consciousness leads to increased collective global consciousness - Introspection, research, and personal growth increase consciousness. As we grow, so grows our consciousness. We've created a chart to reference the levels of growth as seen here:

Level of emotional/ conscious development	Roles playing	Positive Aspects (Growth accomplished at each level)	Negative Aspects (Aspect that needs to be removed to get to the next level)
1- Emotionally closed and fearful	Self-serving survival: control, greed, ruled by fear and insecurity	Motivated mainly by financial security	Manipulative, aggressive, compulsive, and rude
2 - Unaware, needy, relies on others for a sense of self	Social conformity: banding with others for survival	Seeks safety in family and friendships. Values rules & roles	Judgmental, critical, blaming, jealousy, revenge
3 - Self-centered awareness	Ego: self-centered, false sense of confidence	Self-reliant	Arrogant, pride, conceit, superiority discrimination
4 - Emergent as emotionally self-aware	Transitioning: moving into personal empowerment	Acceptance and love of self and others	NA
5 - Self-Actualizing	Internally aligned: balance	neutrality, trust, no expectation of outcome	NA
6 - Enlightenment	Minimalist: servant philanthropist	Inner wisdom, deep inner peace, freedom	NA
7 - Highest level of consciousness	Observer: Non-duality	Bliss, serenity, joy, state of flow	NA

CONSCIOUSNESS IS UNDER THE RUBBLE

Before we conclude let's take a bit of time to reflect on what we've learned with a few last questions for you to journal about: How do you now understand the purpose of emotions in your day-to-day life?

How have you been able to increase your ability to manage your own emotions?

What awareness have you gained around your emotional triggers?

How willing are you to release your subconscious from its position as a security guard?

How willing are you to unpack your own emotional baggage?

How can you see these tools improving your life and your relationships?

Are you interested in raising your own level of consciousness?

Author's notes: More than one Penny!

As Vincent and I were writing this, we were both excited by our shared experiences and the discussions we had about our own (continuing) personal growth journeys. It was our intention to be encouraging as we wrote but I am certain there were times when we became over exuberant. So, if there are parts of the book (or all of it!) that sounds a bit more than just encouraging, it's because of our passion. It's because of how much more amazing we both feel about ourselves, others, and life due to our journeys. It's also because we've both tried a lot of things that didn't work. We are excited to continue our own growth as well as creating tools to share with others.

Moving Ahead

Our hope is that the work we've shared here will have a profound impact on your lives. Understanding emotions and understanding ourselves changes our footprint in the world. It changes how we show up for ourselves and those around us.

Once you begin to unpack the subconscious and the day-to-day emotions are not as weighty then you can manage current emotions more effectively because they are not tied to any of the old painful events. We both want to sincerely thank you for reading this book. It's been an honor to share this work and these experiences with each of you. We hope you have both embraced and enjoyed the material. Together, we truly can change the entire planet, one level of consciousness at a time!

Challenge questions.

The priority challenge. List the percentage of importance do you assign each (total 100%)?

Outwardly: Financial means, social status. %

Social: Close secure connections, healthy relationships.%

Inwardly: Freedom, inner peace, happiness, joy, mindfulness. %

The change or gain challenge. List 2 things you want to change or gain that are not immediate. Examples would be:

Something you feel a lack of movement in.

That one thing that your mind you keep telling yourself you have to do.

More of something: wealth, possessions, security, time, freedom, happiness, peace.

The if money didn't matter challenge.

How would you spend your time? What type of environment would you choose to live in? How might your relationships be different?

The passion project challenge.

What is the one thing you dream about accomplishing the most?

The big hug challenge. Close your eyes. Think of the one person at any point of your life who made you feel the greatest and/or had the most impact on your life.

Who is that person?

Make a list the reasons why.

The emotional self-awareness challenge.

How often do you check in with yourself emotionally during each day?

Can you tell the difference when you are reacting or responding?

Are you aware when you are being triggered? What percentage of the time would you consider your decisions to be conscious choices?

How aware of you of avoidant coping techniques you may be utilizing?

How often to you allow yourself to rest without feeling guilty?

Are you able to create a safe space to compose and process as needed?

Quick Reference Vocabulary Guide

Self-awareness conscious knowledge of your own existence in terms of character, feelings, motives, and desires.

Emotional awareness/emotional self-awareness is the ability to assess how you feel internally and the ability to use emotions to navigate situations. It is the ability to recognize your effect on others around you by recognizing their levels of awareness. The deeper levels of awareness you attain, the more conscious and present you will remain in each moment.

Self-directed/self-efficacy as it relates to this book is an individual's ability to take ownership of their actions and know how to execute the necessary steps to achieve specific goals and objectives. In addition, the individual knows when to seek out support and resources when necessary.

Subconscious as referred to in this material, has taken on the role of the protector. The subconscious diverts our focus when it encounters triggering moments, pushing us to seek the safety of our comfort zone. The subconscious is the cause of the behaviors we've been unable to explain until now.

Triggers are the painful land-minds that are embedded in our emotional fields that cause us to explode internally and react externally when they are designated by a similar experience of the past that needs resolution.

CONSCIOUSNESS IS UNDER THE RUBBLE

Daily Drama is our term for the many things we get caught up in or deem more important than need be.

Core Root Cause - The heart of the dysfunction

Suggested Readings.

Dismissing and Diminishing Your Past Keeps You from Healing by Annie Wright LMFT

3 Problems Caused by Ignoring Your Emotions by Jonice Webb Ph. D.

The New Psychology of Embodied Emotional Intelligence by Patrick De Vleeschauwer Drs.

12 Questions to Test Your Self-Connection by Arash Emamzedeh

The Effects of Self-Centered Parenting on Children by Christine B. L. Adams M.D.

References

Atlas, G. (2022). Emotional Inheritance: A Therapist, Her Patients, and the Legacy of Trauma.

Bessel a. van der Kolk (2015). The Body Keeps the Score: Brain, Mind, and Body in the Healing of Trauma.

Goleman (2005). Emotional Intelligence: Why It Can Matter More Than IQ.

Grow, Gerald O. (1991/1996). "Teaching Learners to be Self-Directed." Adult Education Quarterly, 41 (3), 125-149. Expanded version available online at: <http://www.longleaf.net/ggrow>.

Guglielmino, L. (1978). Development of the self- directed learning readiness scale. (Doctoral dissertation, University of Georgia, 1977). Dissertation Abstracts International, 38, 6467A.

Hyland, N. & Kranzow, J. (2011). Faculty and Student Views of Using Digital Tools to Enhance Self-Directed Learning and Critical Thinking. International Journal of Self Directed Learning, 8 (2), 11 – 22.

Knowles, M. (1975). Self-Directed Learning: A Guide for Learners and Teachers. New York, NY. Association Press.

Lane, R. D., & Schwartz, G. E. (1987). Levels of emotional awareness: A cognitive-developmental theory and its application to psychopathology. The American Journal of Psychiatry, 144(2), 133–143.

Ruskan, J. (2006) Emotional Clearing: An East / West Guide to
Releasing Negative Feelings and Awakening Unconditional
Happiness

Smith, R., Killgore, W. D. S., & Lane, R. D. (2018). The structure
of emotional experience and its relation to trait emotional
awareness: A theoretical review. Emotion, 18(5), 670–692.
https://doi.org/10.1037/emo0000376

Saarni, C. (1999). The Development of Emotional Competence.
Guilford Press.

Books By This Author

Unpacking Emotional Baggage

A personal story of triumph over the childhood trauma and the eating addiction associated with the trauma. An extraordinarily true story about getting down to the truth in a world filled with distractions.

When the illusion of a picture-perfect life was shattered by a near death experience, one woman set off on a very different type of journey. As her perceived identity and value vanished in an ousting from corporate America she turned inward with humbling resilience.

In an incredible journey that spanned an unprecedented decade removed from the workplace she defies the popular belief that financial security must come first. She navigated complex twists and turns that finally delivered her to a deeply conscious lifestyle. This carefully crafted adventurous romp sparks recognition in us all as we follow her search to make peace with her life-long nemesis: food. She bravely tackles her dysfunctional method of avoidant coping only to uncover a legacy of generational trauma. She then confronts in her one true oppressor, her own subconscious.

Armed with a curious and open mind the writer presents a candidly raw view into the relentless pursuit of personal truth with gut wrenchingly brutal honesty, offering up the ride of a lifetime and perhaps a deeper glimpse inside yourself. Have you ever wondered why you can't control yourself at times? Maybe it's food, drinking, smoking? Or what about retail therapy? Are you wondering what keeps you from living a healthy lifestyle? If you want to get to the core root, this is a must-read book.

Available on Amazon.